Couples Therapy in Managed Care: Facing the Crisis

Barbara Jo Brothers
Editor

Couples Therapy in Managed Care: Facing the Crisis has been co-published simultaneously as *Journal of Couples Therapy*, Volume 8, Numbers 3/4 1999.

Routledge
Taylor & Francis Group
LONDON AND NEW YORK

First published 1999 by
The Haworth Press, Inc

Published 2013 by Routledge
711 Third Avenue, New York, NY, 10017, USA
2 Park Square, Milton Park, Abingdon, Oxon OX14 4RN

Routledge is an imprint of the Taylor & Francis Group, an informa business

Couples Therapy in Managed Care: Facing the Crisis has been
co-published simultaneously as *Journal of Couples Therapy,*
Volume 8, Numbers 3/4 1999.

The development, preparation, and publication of this work has been undertaken with great care. However, the publisher, employees, editors, and agents of The Haworth Press and all imprints of The Haworth Press, Inc., including The Haworth Medical Press® and Pharmaceutical Products Press®, are not responsible for any errors contained herein or for consequences that may ensue from use of materials or information contained in this work. Opinions expressed by the author(s) are not necessarily those of The Haworth Press, Inc.

Cover design by Thomas J. Mayshock Jr.

Library of Congress Cataloging-in-Publication Data

Couples therapy in managed care: facing the crisis/Barbara Jo Brothers, editor.
    p. cm
    "Co-published simultaneously as Journal of couples therapy, Volume 8, Numbers 3/4 1999."
    Includes bibliographical references and index.
    1. Marital psychotherapy. 2 Managed care plans (Medical care) I. Brothers, Barbara Jo, 1940-
RC488.5 .C64385 1999
616.89'156–dc21

                                                   99-051401

ISBN 13: 978-0-789-00823-7 (pbk)

Couples Therapy in Managed Care: Facing the Crisis

CONTENTS

ABOUT THE EDITOR

Barbara Jo Brothers, MSW, BCD, a Diplomate in Clinical Social Work, National Association of Social Workers, is in private practice in New Orleans. She received her BA from the University of Texas and her MSW from Tulane University, where she is currently on the faculty. She was Editor of *The Newsletter of the American Academy of Psychotherapists* from 1976 to 1985, and was Associate Editor of *Voices: The Art and Science of Psychotherapy* from 1979 to 1989. She has 30 years of experience, in both the public and private sectors, helping people to form skills that will enable them to connect emotionally. The author of numerous articles and book chapters on authenticity in human relating, she has advocated healthy, congruent communication that builds intimacy as opposed to destructive, incongruent communication which blocks intimacy. In addition to her many years of direct work with couples and families, Ms. Brothers has led numerous workshops on teaching communication in families and has also played an integral role in the development of training programs in family therapy for mental health workers throughout the Louisiana state mental health system. She is a board member of the Institute for International Connections, a non-profit organization for cross-cultural professional development focused on training and cross-cultural exchange with psychotherapists in Russia, republics once part of what used to be the Soviet Union, and other Eastern European countries.

Preface

We owe the birth of this volume to Norman Shub, gestalt therapist in Cleveland, Ohio. Deeply concerned about the erosion of quality of care for patients at the mercy of the managed care industry, Shub called for a publication on this theme. Then he did the groundwork of finding the authors among a wide range of experts.

Shub keenly feels the responsibility of the mental health profession-al to advocate responsible practice with patients. His own article is submitted as one specific illustration of the managed care Procrustean Bed; he shows damage done by rigidity of application whether it fits with diagnosis or not. In "The Unmanageability of Characterologic Couples in Managed Care," Shub addresses the iatrogenic potential in the following: combination of characterology with brief treatment, the model mandated by managed care companies. In this article, Shub provides just one clear example of how managed care is hazardous to mental health.

The greatest danger of managed care policies may be the subtle influence on *thinking* regarding treatment. In calling for *Couples Therapy in Managed Care*, Norman Shub tugs us back toward remember-ing who we are and what we are about: psychotherapists whose "busi-ness" it is to help human beings enter their own separate worlds of higher functioning. "McMental-Health" flipped out at top speed is not a model that fits all sizes.

I deeply appreciate all the work Norman Shub has done in helping to bring *Couples Therapy in Managed Care* into being.

Barbara Jo Brothers, Editor

From Virgina Satir:
Models of Perceiving the World–
Attitude Toward Change

Virginia Satir

EDITOR'S NOTE. The following is a transcript of one of a series of lectures Avanta Process ommunity Meeting , rested utte, olorado, August and Process ommunity Meeting , August of . They were given during the early part of a day residential seminar they were preceded by demonstrations which illustrated some of these points and followed by demonstrations which illustrated other points. irginia would weave her lectures in among her e ercises and demonstrations so that a tapestry would form, one illustrating the other. he was deliberately creating an optimuum conte t for learning. The lectures were given over a month's time.

ECT RE

. . . Now, we come to the fourth thing which is the attitude toward change. For people who hold that relationships are 1 in some form of dominance and submission and 2 use conformity and obedience to define themselves and 3 who look for the one right way, then what they have to do with change is stop it as much as possible, because change means going into the unknown and we must not do that. We must always keep "what is right," here, where we know it.

This lecture transcript is part of a series that appears in past and subsequent issues of the *Journal of Couples Therapy.*

[Haworth co-indexing entry note]: "From Virginia Satir: Models of Perceiving the World–Attitude Toward Change." Satir, Virginia. Co-published simultaneously in *Journal of Couples Therapy* (The Haworth Press, Inc.) Vol. 8, No. 3/4, 1999, pp. 1-5; and: *Couples Therapy in Managed Care: Facing the Crisis* (ed: Barbara Jo Brothers) The Haworth Press, Inc., 1999, pp. 1-5.

The whole thrust in this is to stop change or make it as little as possible. Change becomes an extraordinary thing that must be guarded against. So, when a kid becomes adolescent and wants to dress in different clothes, someone has a heart attack. Or, if any kind of change takes place. Changing the way you look or changing the way you talk or any kind of change gets scary within this kind of frame. The minute, then, that something is changing, what has to happen immediately, which you know about, are the defenses have to be there.

That is one of the reasons why it is so important to have support groups for change. Otherwise, we get into that kind of trouble, because these people feel, people who do this feel, that their security is based in keeping the status quo. "Don't rock the boat, keep the status quo." The efforts here are to maintain status quo and that, then, feels like safety. You know from what I talked to you about in the change process, maintaining a status quo, of course means you can't go anywhere. But, if you do go somewhere, you have to do it out of guilt. You have to make believe like you don't own it. You have to project it on somebody else. You know how that goes. The guilt: "Well, I shouldn't have done it." Or, "You made me do it." Or "I really wasn't there when it was happening, even though I was."

We have to do all kinds of funny things that have negative implications for moving and changing. Once we say that change is bad, then any way we deal with it, we also have to call bad. Look around in the families, look around in international relations, look around anywhere. People, I think, get mixed up that homeostasis means "no change." Homeostasis simply means "a new balance." No new balance is going to happen unless we go through all the stages of change. You will find this over and over again. That is why I said maybe it will become a little clearer to you that your triads, and then, indeed, your condo's residence during the seminar , anywhere you find people, is the place for taking a look at what will surface. I am amazed over and over again that I keep finding things that come up that I get a chance to look at. What I like about me at this point is I don't push that away anymore; I look at it.

We were helpless when we came into the world. We had to depend upon who was around us and we still don't know are not consciously aware of all the stuff that we learned. It keeps popping up. That is why in this seminar, I try to make as many structures as I can that are going to allow us to take new looks at where we are. Because, actually, if I say to somebody, "I know that you don't want to go into the unknown, that you don't want to change," they won't say, "That's right." They will say, "I'm afraid to." They will say, "What will happen if I do?" And, they will tell me more about how it is too much for them. That is why all the support and the trust and the willingness to move and to try out things is so important. And, that is why, for somebody to say–"Oh, if you will just stop what you are doing, everything would be fine"–doesn't work. It doesn't work that way.

The world is in this space. Psychology has been in this space since psychology emerged as a discipline . It is not very old. Human relations have been in this space because this is all the world knew for so long. That doesn't leave out the fact that there were people with good hearts. There were people with wonderful intentions. But, just like up here gestures toward blackboard where threat and reward model is juxtaposed with seed and growth model , I had to keep those things inside. I didn't dare talk about it. If I'm grown up, I shouldn't talk about my doubts, etc.

When this last century came to an end, just prior to that, we began with, what I consider to be the first seed to what we can do now which came with Freud: the discovery that inside we have the ability to change and that change can be destructive or constructive. We don't have to wait for the outside to change . This idea that change must come from the outside is thousands of years old, entrenched, very entrenched.

ECT RE

. . . the last one of the four phenomenon which have to do with people and their interrelationship with one another has to do with attitude change

Every once in a while, I smile because people talk as though change is something that they legislate. It's so funny; I say to myself . . . I don't say it out loud because I time what I say out loud. But when I think about it, change is constant. There is no such thing as we can wait for change. There's no such thing. So what is the attitude toward change (p. 35)?

. . . Now let's get to the attitude toward change . . . People who tend to have a relationship in a hierarchy, who treat themselves as not always quite up to snuff, who try to explain events by stereotypes also are trying to freeze change. Freeze it. First of all, look at it as abnormal. It's abnormal. And what you do is allow as little as possible. And all the energy is going towards maintaining the status quo. If any of you have tried to work with people who have difficult problems, you will see how there is an effort to hang onto what is at present. You notice that? The status quo is that which is known, It has no relationship to comfort, but to what is known, And if there's ever a question between comfort and familiarity, familiarity will almost always win out.

This is the essence of your resistance here too. They the "resisting" clients know what the current present is, it's familiar. They don't know what's out there. And so that which you see is somebody trying to hang onto something–this what you call resistance. I respect it, because I know how hard it is to go from the familiar, even if I think there's something comfortable out there. And you must know that too–the risk-taking that is involved with going from someplace you know to something you don't know . . .

So, the energy then, and security for the self rests on maintaining the status quo within this kind of frame. Security rests on the maintaining the status quo. That means that the balance, in a systems principle, balance has been achieved . . . Remember, every system is in balance. The question is what price does each part pay to stay in that balance? So it's never anything out of balance, but it's what price does each piece pay. And it is with people who are living their lives like this, it's the best they know, the prices are very high. In disease, in lack of intimacy, guilt, in their lack of productivity, and creativity, their lack of joy in life. Very high.

Now that's my picture of how most of the world is going on. I know many people who have hopes but they can't really have their hopes validated. It's getting a little better, but most people have not known how they could do differently (p. 64-65).

. . . Now, lets come down to the next part of the attitude toward change. People who . . . do take risks . . . who go into this part as opposed to those of do not , of course, see change as, first of all, that it *is*. It exists, and that it is essential and that it is inevitable. And because it is so, it becomes acknowledged and everybody knows that the very fact of change means going into the unknown. You cannot have change without taking a step from the known to the unknown. There is no way you can do it.

As soon as you go into the unknown, you are taking a risk. And the risk that you are taking is that you will meet something you haven't met before. How many of you had children before you had children? Or had spouses before you had spouses or were fourteen before you were fourteen? None of you. No matter how much somebody told you before you got married how it was going to be, you were in for a few surprises. That's not good or bad. It simply means if you haven't been there before, you haven't had the experience. And the nature of life is that change is going on all the time so we're always going to the unknown.

So in a way we have deluded ourselves to say there is such a thing as safety or security based on keeping the status quo. It can't happen. That is where I think our cancer comes. We've got some pretty good evidence for that, about people who are full of wanting to do on all levels down to the cells, but have rules about themselves that they mustn't, so the energy has got to go someplace. An energy that doesn't have a place has to go to someplace else. So the person who can rage and someone who can say, "feel your rage and let the rage come," doesn't have to usually translate it into murder. But the one who says, "You have no business being angry with me. That's not your job. What did I do to you?" This person, on the other hand, would be stopping the health-giving, natural, energy flow.

Now, this means that in this frame, that security is based on risk-taking and by the nature of it has to be . . . the security is based on the certainty of uncertainty. Now that sounds like double talk, but I don't believe it is. So uncertainty, ambiguity, are all part of this. Have any of you ever experimented with making the right decision? You always know afterwards whether it fit or not even remotely, didn't you? Those of you who can say, "Hey, I did the best that I could and now I'll learn from this and go on," were able to live with uncertainty that maybe it wouldn't be right and then could go on and see if you could get a little closer . . . to right (p. 74-76).

 . . . People often tell me they have no choice. Well, I know what they're telling me. They don't see any choices, but they don't, in and of themselves, experience the wide range of choices that people have all the time, and these choices have something to do with how people feel their self-esteem . . .

 . . . And that is what I teach the people who come to me for help, is how to take those little steps that open the little doors. It's the cracks in life that open up to the other, it's not the big windows. And a lot of people have to have a lot of help to do that . . . (p. 77).

Nothing Is "Here to Stay"

Barbara Jo Brothers

For a long time, all discussions of the evils and burdens of managed care always seemed to end with, "Managed Care is 'Here to Stay.'" The main problem with making such as statement is it helps the current unsavory reality stay in place via self-reinforcement. The belief system of the speaker is reinforced by the speech.

Folks, nothing is here to stay. Change is life. All things come to an end. During the time period in which this volume was being assembled, there has been a growing rumble of dissatisfaction with managed care as we have come to know it. For decades, the American public resisted socialized medicine out of that dread of loss of choice of physician. While nobody was looking, managed care–private industry, no less–slipped in and snatched that unfettered choice away before people knew what was happening.

The problems are in the paradigm. There are conflicting interests between the merchant mentality and serving the sick. A former patient of mine, subsequently employed by a managed care company, talked about his genuine concern for meeting the needs of the callers, adding, in a tone somewhere between apology and guilt, "But I know it is a business . . ." It was as if he had to stop and remind himself that the number of sessions he might mercifully mete out to a given client came at a cost to his company.

The patient is urged to think of herself/himself as consumer. In fact, some social agencies have re-named their clientele to that effect. In this frame, an HMO works fine as long as one does not get sick or

[Haworth co-indexing entry note]: "*Nothing* Is 'Here to Stay.'" Brothers, Barbara Jo. Co-published simultaneously in *Journal of Couples Therapy* (The Haworth Press, Inc.) Vol. 8, No. 3/4, 1999, pp. -8; and: *Couples Therapy in Managed Care: Facing the Crisis* (ed: Barbara Jo Brothers) The Haworth Press, Inc., 1999, pp. -8. Single or multiple copies of this article are available for a fee from The Haworth ocument elivery Service [1-8 -34 -9 8, 9: a.m. - 5: p.m. (ST). -mail address: getinfo haworthpressinc. com].

plans carefully and methodically ahead for the kind of illness or therapy situation which they may, in the future, need. The "buyer" is in no position to bargain-hunt while experiencing either a serious physical or emotional pain. Yet the managed care intake personnel on the other end of the phone line is dickering–dollar signs in mind–with sessions and types of providers to be granted.

Although it seems obvious, the peril in mindless use of the business model in health and mental health care is that, almost by definition, the theme shifts from persons to profits. Patient–or "consumer"–needs is not the priority; profit is. My former patient said as much–he had to remember, "It's a business." The other "health hazard" in this change of model: in the business world, manipulation is a time-honored, well used tool. In the hands of a psychotherapist, it becomes a dangerous weapon.

However, the winds seem to be shifting these days. Apparently, "rewarding" people with cheaper doctor bills does not seem to result in their needing fewer services. *ew rleans ity siness* notes "HMO's are experiencing tough times across the board . . . large players . . . have posted disappointing earnings reports, and horror stories about denied care have caused a public backlash" (Russell, 1998, p. 37). An *lletin* quotes, "A Washington Post/ABC News poll taken in July . . . found 6 percent of Americans favoring tougher government regulation of managed care organizations" (Gapay, 1998, p. 18).

Perhaps, these entrepreneurs, whose bottom lines have begun to sink to new levels, will move on to more lucrative ventures. Faced with less money and more accountability, they may begin to return the healing of bodies and souls back toward those more interested in service to humankind than in turning a buck.

Managed care, in its current form, may *not* be here to stay.

REFERENCES

apay, . (September, 1998). Showdown looms on patient rights. *AARP Bulletin ol 3* , No. 8. American Association of etired Persons, 601 E St. N.W., Washington, D.C.

ussell, J. (March 9, 1998). oad ahead is rocky and steep for most HMOs. *New Orleans City Business.* New Orleans, ouisiana: New Orleans Publishing roup.

Is Multi-Generational Work Gone or Here to Stay? Working in a Managed Care Environment

C. Jesse Carlock

SUMMARY. Multi-generational therapy is here to stay if we "work smart." Managed care, with its ever-widening stranglehold on services, has had a tremendous impact on the practice of psychotherapy. All but those therapists treating the elite have been forced to take a position relative to managed care. The author suggests that those therapists who choose to work within the managed care arena develop creative strate- gems to play the managed care game while holding true to personal values and the integrity of their approach to behavior change. Practical ways to "work smart" and utilize managed care to the clients' best advantage are suggested. *Article copies availa le for a fee from The Haworth Document Delivery Service: 8 34 678. E mail address: getinfo haworthpressinc.com e site: http: www.haworthpressinc.com*

KEYWORDS. Managed care, multi-generational therapy, genogram, psychoeducational

The value which best captures the essence of managed care is expediency. Insistence on brief therapy, the briefer the better, is

C. Jesse Carlock, PhD, is a psychologist in practice in Dayton, Ohio, training coordinator for the estalt Institute of Central Ohio in Columbus, and Associate Clinical Professor with the School of Professional Psychology at Wright State Uni- versity. She is author of the upcoming third edition of *Enhancing Self Esteem.*

[Haworth co-indexing entry note]: "Is Multi- enerational Wor one or Here to Stay Wor ing in a Managed Care nvironment." Carloc , C. Jesse. Co-published simultaneously in *Journal of Couples Therapy* (The Haworth Press, Inc.) Vol. 8, No. 3/4, 1999, pp. 9- 3; and: *Couples Therapy in Managed Care: Facing the Crisis* (ed: Barbara Jo Brothers) The Haworth Press, Inc., 1999, pp. 9- 3. Single or multiple copies of this article are available for a fee from The Haworth ocument elivery Service [1-8 -34 -9 8, 9: a.m. - 5: p.m. (ST). -mail address: getinfo haworthpressinc.com].

viewed as the "golden road" to cost containment and increased profits for managed care companies. To some, multi-generational couples therapy would seem no longer viable and practitioners of these approaches, along with practitioners of psychoanalysis and other long-term, depth therapy approaches, should be relegated to an archaic category of obsolescent theories. On the contrary, multi-generational approaches such as Bowenian and Satirian models tend to be efficient and precise in the hands of experienced, well-trained professionals and can be adapted to meet the time demands that managed care imposes.

While a singular emphasis on symptom reduction runs counter to many therapists' values of producing deeper, long lasting, and more pervasive change, and recognizing the importance of the therapeutic relationship, symptom reduction is, nonetheless also a value of any theoretical approach. The challenge is to find ways to meet our equally important other objectives.

Virginia Satir would often caution her trainees about asking dichotomous questions such as, "Is multi-generational work gone or here to stay?" She would shift the question in a variety of ways such as: When is multi-generational appropriate? nder what conditions can we use this approach? How can multi-generational approach be employed given the current resources? How can we change the context, the time frame, or other variables to meet our objectives and stay true to our values? These kinds of questions mobilize our creativity and our intellect.

Recently, when I spoke with Betty Carter (personal communication, May, 1997) about the question posed in the title of this article, she responded: "This question is equivalent to asking, "Is surgery gone or here to stay" or "Is the Cat Scan gone or here to stay?"" After all, your theory is your theory. If it has demonstrated utility, of course it is here to stay. But managed care is here to stay also, at least for the foreseeable future.

I work in a private practice setting. Since I choose to serve a client base of varying socio-economic levels and many of my clients cannot afford to self-pay, I decided to be flexible and find creative ways to work within the limitations imposed by managed care. While these restrictions do not provide an ideal playing field, I have been successful in working the system to the clients' best advantage. While operating within the symptom focused demands of managed care (I, too want to reduce symptoms), I keep my own additional foci as well, which are addressing the underlying issues driving the symptoms and helping individuals and couples to flower. I am now part of a therapy underground, for I have not given up the value I place on growth and the value of altering underlying patterns of symptomology. The challenge has been to adapt the therapy design while staying true to my basic values and my theoretical frame. But I'm a realist too, so I do what I can do working within the constraints of the resources.

ANA ED CARE
ENE R ARTNER

While I see managed care representatives as formidable opponents, some more formidable than others, treating them as the enemy is unproductive. My approach has been to find ways to work with these people so that I can at least partially meet my objectives while using their frames and speaking their language. The way to do this is through subterfuge. It is a losing battle to try to convince managed care that my deeper goals are valuable, but in order to preserve my integrity, I have found ways to incorporate what I value even within the limitations managed care imposes. Since my core values are at the heart of my approach, I must stay true to my basic values while playing within their rules. These basic values also include behaving in an ethical manner and protecting myself legally.

As Nevis (1997, p. 11) notes, "Psychological practice such as Gestalt therapy and organizational development consultation, is strongly influenced by social, economic, political, and intellectual development." Economic factors are now driving changes in overall mental health care. Since behavior change is still valued, though emasculated by economic forces, I have come to accept that part of my work must now go underground. In order to preserve what I value, I have developed strategies to deal with managed care in order to accomplish my objectives.

Though not ideal, for I prefer being up front and open, I have found that by employing thoughtful stratagems, I can preserve my most strongly held values and continue my work with a fairly broad spectrum of people. But it is not possible to achieve these covert goals if managed care representatives are treated as the "enemy" and we embattle ourselves and engage in overt power struggles. I've witnessed too many colleagues go that route and lose miserably. They are extruded from panels and can no longer serve clients over whom the battle grew nor can they now treat any other clients who are under this mental health plan. I would not claim this as a victory, for me or the client. Yet, neither is succumbing palatable. If I am to advocate effectively for a client covert tactics are essential. Straightforwardness can work also if used with good judgement, always assessing the likely impact on the relationship between you and the managed care representative and ultimately, you and the client. In essence, we must treat the managed care representative as any other difficult client whom we are committed to treat.

R IN   IT IN ANA ED CARE
AT D ES IT TA E

When working within a multitude of managed care systems, it is imperative that at the onset of therapy the couples' resources for therapy be determined. This would include an examination of the scope and limits of the couple's insurance benefits, the restrictions placed by the particular managed care system, as well as the couples' attitudes towards and capacity to fund a fee for service payment contract to continue therapy once their limited benefits are exhausted.

The expectations of managed care companies are similar in their emphasis on brief therapy, but their definitions of brief therapy can differ considerably depending on the company managing the contracts as well as on the particular employer. Contract coverage ranges from crisis intervention and stabilization to symptom resolution to medical necessity. No one as yet has adequately defined "medical necessity." Some will provide 2 or more sessions if treatment can be justified; others provide as few as six sessions. I use various simple outcome measures that fall in the public domain to track key symptoms. I use the results of these measures to help justify continued treatment and to demonstrate treatment progress. Clients respond well to these measures as they provide quantitative evidence of their progress. Treatment reviewers appreciate the concrete data also.

My office manager spends a great deal of time up front clarifying contract terms and limitations so we all are aware of the "playing field" and can make intelligible decisions as to whether we will proceed. We carefully go over the terms and limitations with the client so they are clear. Provided with only the barest of facts about policy provisions at the time of policy choice, if in fact they are offered a choice, most often employees have been misled by the scanty information provided. For example, information provided to the client may indicate a maximum of 2 or even 4 sessions per year, but, in fact, many fewer sessions will ever be approved due to "medical necessity" clauses or "crisis intervention and stabilization" clauses. Also, the maximum number of sessions may also include psychiatric consults for medication evaluation and medication checks. A careful reworking of client expectations is necessary. If they are dissatisfied with the provisions, we discuss options of continuation as a self-pay client or advise the client regarding other insurance options if their employers provide a choice. Sadly, most employees are not savvy and frequently regret the choices they have made. As a result, this Fall, prior to insurance enrollment time, we are offering an educational session for our clients providing them with the inside story of the various insurance plans and managed care parameters, including information on what questions to ask, and what to look for when they evaluate any options provided.

Once we have defined the approximate range we must work within, the clients and I then formulate the treatment plan with goals which are achievable within that time frame. I translate the goals into language that case managers can hear. I also look at the therapy process, particularly when resources are limited, in units of work. We might complete one unit of work now, clients terminate and attempt to further integrate the learnings, then resume therapy at a later date and complete another unit. During the therapy interims, the couple can be plugged into whatever community resources are available and comply with whatever else might be included in their maintenance plan. In essence, I have learned how to maximize the benefits of the revolving door.

My basic theoretical frame is a weaving of the Satirian intergeneration approach and the Gestalt approach which are highly complementary. I am also versed in Bowenian theory which is also complementary to Satir's approach. From the beginning of my career, I have regularly invested in intensive training to hone my skills and expand my knowledge base. In general, the more skillful therapists are in any theoretical orientation, the easier it will be to survive in the managed care environment.

ASSESS ENT

As with other approaches, assessment begins with the first phone call when I and my office staff are already assessing patterns, dynamics, and levels of emotional reactivity. In the waiting room, as I watch how clients relate to office staff or other clients should interactions occur, and early in the first session I continue to observe dynamics and develop hypotheses. I have trained office staff to observe patterns and feed me information on what they observe as they relate with clients regarding business matters or observe them in the waiting room or in the parking lot. This information is enormously revealing as the couple tends to be less guarded around non-clinical staff.

In the early part of the first session I listen as partners relate what they want from the therapy process, carefully observe both their individual and interactive processes. I also discuss ground rules and my expectations of them regarding homework assignments. Homework assignments are extremely important in areas such as data gathering, awareness building, increasing emotional ownership of behavior and its impact on self and other, tracking progress on specific goals, instituting changes, and experimenting with new behavior. Completion of homework assignments is part of the therapy contract. The constraints of managed care often serve to keep the couple and me focused and motivated and I want to reinforce their responsibilities as partners in the process. By being clear about ground rules related to such matters as one partner's lateness or absence, phone calls, outside contacts, confidentiality, homework and the like, I can help avert unnecessary tangles and triangulation.

The three generational genogram is the backbone of this model. Like x-rays, EKGs and the like, the genogram is a diagnostic tool for multi-generational couples work. nlike more specific medical diagnostic procedures, genograms display a broad range of information which may be interpreted from a number of different theoretical perspectives (Rohrbaugh, Rogers, and McGoldrick, 1992). The whole process of genogram construction also differs from medical diagnostic procedures. The genogram is usually constructed in partnership with the couple within the therapy session. Although computer generated genograms are available (Gerson, 1985) most therapists prefer to gather information and complete the construction within therapy sessions in order to avoid missing valuable affective information which increases awareness of important tender spots which may need further probing and attention. Those who do use the computerized genogram often use it after interviewing to create an orderly, clear picture of the family system for each participant.

As Gerson and McGoldrick (1986) explain, the genogram provides an efficient summary which can be updated continually as the larger picture develops. The genogram is also an interpretive tool. Indeed, it is very useful in generating hypotheses and in providing information useful in reframing issues at hand. Once hypotheses are formed based on the presenting problems and patterns, roles, beliefs, and dynamics observed directly by the therapist, the genogram can then by focused on retrieving vital information related the these themes as well as on emphasizing individual and systemic strengths.

Through the process of genogram construction, rapport is established and partners are helped to adopt a more systemic position, moving them away from a who is "right" and who is "wrong" blaming focus to looking at each partner's personal responsibility for individual contributions to the problems in the relationship. Each partner is invited to join the therapist in what Satir (1991) characterized as the "control tower" position, to view the current marital problems in a broader historical perspective bringing to light roots of current behavior derived from the family of origin and the extended family. The intergenerational approach through the construction of three generational genograms is transformed into a tool to create psychological distance and reduce emotional reactivity, diffusing anxiety and blame in the couple system. The genogram helps reorient the couple away from petty arguments towards identifying the underlying issues" (Carter, personal communication, May 5, 1997). This streamlines the entire therapy process. As partners are able to view their current problems as embedded in a larger context, partners are often able to develop mutual respect and acceptance (Gerson, Hoffman, Sauls, lrici, 1993).

By formulating the genogram through a dialogical process, the therapist can begin to determine the "hot" areas and determine which of these areas should be elaborated or deferred (Gerson et al., 1993). Reframing, making new connections to broaden awareness, and shifting perspectives can also begin immediately. According to a leading Satirian therapist, Banmen (personal communication, June 18, 1997), "The biggest limitation of having clients do much of this (constructing the genogram) alone is that they focus on the content and I am interested in the impact the content has had on them." A thorough discussion of genograms and their interpretations may be found in McGoldrick and Gerson (1985).

Another valuable opportunity genograms provide is to help "surface the strengths that can be reharnessed for present growth" (Banmen, personal communication, June 18, 1997). Heightening the couples' awareness of their strengths is often neglected when the couple and the therapist become fixated on problem areas. Yet couples are often unaware of their strengths. Satir repeatedly drilled into her trainees the importance of identifying and expanding strengths and using them as resources to manage the problem areas. Knowing ones' strengths as a couple also stimulates hope. Couples need to know what they do well in order to instill hope and pride and so that couples can use these strengths with awareness to effect changes in problem areas.

After gathering basic genogram information and observing the partners' reactions, hypothesis building and goal formulation can be more finely tuned. I ask myself, how can I focus the work, given the anticipated time frame, to maximally benefit this client system? Any further exploration of the extended family system is then focused around these identified major themes and patterns (both positive and negative). The couple and therapist are partners in this process of jointly forming the specific goals of the treatment sequence.

While constructing much of the genogram within sessions, I often give clients homework assignments between sessions related to the major themes and patterns which have become figural through the genogram exploration. I might request that partners track down further information, locate family stories, interview family members, or gather family pictures related to the identified and agreed upon themes and patterns. These homework assignments can help reduce the time spent in sessions reaching for details long forgotten or unknown. This information is then processed carefully within the session. I find that involving couples outside of sessions in such assignments increases their involvement and motivation.

Additionally, the genogram provides a map to help the couple keep in mind contributions of other family members, family patterns, events, family beliefs, and faulty coping strategies and defensive patterns developed in the family of origin which fuel the current marital/ couple problems. Transgenerational strengths may also be highlighted. The genogram is useful in helping the couple "find the context in which (the) coping has developed" (J. Banmen, personal communication, June 18, 1997). When clients become interested in the genogram process they often reveal an enormous amount of personal material that might otherwise take months to surface. Anxiety is reduced since the individual is defocused and attention is shifted to the dynamics, coping styles and beliefs of the broader family. The therapeutic ground is thereby greatly enriched. As intergenerational patterns are identified, the genogram may also stimulate motivation to change. As can be seen, the genogram construction process is useful in providing an avenue to accomplish many of the numerous tasks of the beginning phase simultaneously. The genogram sets the stage and helps identify the broad strokes of the work ahead.

Through this initial phase, primary diadic patterns such as closeness and distance, power and control, overfunctioning and underfunctioning, and conflict patterns are identified and tied to interactional patterns in the extended family of origin. Deeper work to heighten awareness of and shift these patterns can now begin.

In assessing stressors, Carter and McGoldrick (1988) recommend evaluating the level of anxiety flowing in a family by examining two principle sources of stressors: vertical and horizontal. Vertical stressors are comprised of patterns of relating passed down through the generations primarily through emotional triangling in myths, themes, roles, taboos, secrets, rules, attitudes, expectations, and loaded issues (Carter and McGoldrick, 1988). According to Carter and McGoldrick, 1988), horizontal stressors include those sources of anxiety couples experience as they move through the couple life cycle (transitions, losses, unpredictable events, illnesses, disabilities, war, economic downturns). When anxiety from both vertical and horizontal stressors intersect, intense stress will result.

Betty Carter (personal communication, May 5, 1997) also emphasizes the importance of examining the broader socio-political aspects of the couple. Carter helps couples to determine how much power each partner's status (gender, race, ethnicity, sexual orientation, class) provides or does not provide, and to examine how that status plays out in the relationship and in the world. Carter then attempts to move the couple on the same side against the problem. Carter (personal communication, May 5, 1997) believes that in our present culture, demands of jobs have displaced connection to community, neighborhood and religion and couples are often socially isolated. Couples' use of time and degree of work involvement, therefore, also need to be assessed. Carter (personal communication, May 5, 1997) and her colleagues also look at how these socio-political factors can lead to violence and aggression in couples.

The family therapy literature, notes Gerson et al. (1993), shows that common interactional dynamics can be culled from the multiple problems couples present such as:

- closeness-distance (pursuer-distancer)
- overresponsibility-underresponsibility
- blaming-placating

Satir often reduced the principal issues played out between partners to three: intimacy, power, and self-esteem. Work, parenting, money, in-laws, religion, and sex are the primary battlegrounds.

S C   ED CATI NA   R   S

Satir (1991), Carter (personal communication, May 5, 1997), and Guerin et al. (1987) all favor the use of psychoeducational programs as a prerequisite to therapy or to augment the therapy as it proceeds. Decisions about the timing of placement in the program will depend on the degree to which the couple is embroiled in conflict and the degree of trust and good will operating in the system. If emotional reactiveness is high and good will is low, it is likely the partners will use concepts learned as part of their armament.

If properly timed, however, psychoeducational groups can help deepen and speed progress as they are efficient and cost-effective ways to orient clients to a variety of relevant concepts such as:

- Developmental stages of couples and families
- Genograms: A three generational perspective
- Rules, roles, myths, and rituals
- Conflict styles
- Pursuer-distancer patterns
- Stress stances, dances and self-esteem
- Triangles
- Ingredients of an interaction
- Couples "Parts Parties"

- Race, ethnicity, gender, class, sexual orientation, and power
- The impact of technology on the couple systems
- Making contact
- Strengthening resource networks

In addition to advancing the therapy process, such programs provide a context where couples can network with other couples reducing isolation, providing perspective and awareness of common problems which couples face, and offering opportunities to expand social networks.

Feasibility of such psychoeducational programs, however, primarily depends on having a large enough client base from which to draw participants without having to spend large of amounts of time and money advertising and marketing them. In general, they are most practical when associated with larger practices or networks of smaller practices where multiple therapists will refer to these programs.

E INNIN   ASE   TREAT ENT

After the assessment phase the next set of sessions involves, at least in the conflict-ridden couple, further work to stop the petty and unproductive arguing. As Betty Carter (personal communication, May 5, 1997) so simply puts it, "I teach them how to close their mouths and establish the (safe, calm) emotional climate." Of course, the therapist must work throughout the therapy to maintain this climate. Then the heart of the work can begin.

The underlying issues which have been identified are now brought to the forefront. Efforts in this phase may be made to identify the unique strengths of the couple system, identify and strengthen outside support of the couple system, teach basic communication and negotiation skills, begin to heighten awareness of and gradually begin to break problematic patterns of fusion, distance, or conflict and establish greater differentiation between partners. Other goals might involve beginning steps to rebalance power and bring more equity into the relationship, or, in the case of a detached couple system, foster communication of the unspoken and begin to bridge the gap between the partners. Whatever the issue or theme being worked, attention is given to each partner's reciprocal steps in their unique dance.

Sculpting the essential relationship dynamics is highly illuminating as is sculpting the relationship dynamics in each partner's family of origin as well as the extended family dynamics on both maternal and paternal sides. Sculpting brings the genogram to life and in so doing increases the ability of partners to step in and out of the observer role, increases both cognitive and emotional awareness and provides a vehicle for generating possibilities for change. Virginia Satir taught me to think in pictures (sculptures and scenes) and to give form to these pictures with the assistance and active participation of clients. With a variety of technical skills, creativity, intuition, presence, and contact, couples can be helped both to experience, with dramatic intensity, the core of their impasse and to view with nascent detachment (Satir's "control tower" position) the current relationship pattern and, in a broader context, the family legacy of those motifs. For what is important in this phase is for each partner to begin to take ownership and responsibility, both cognitively and emotionally, for the particular relationship dance they have co-created. It is always a duet. One partner can change the dance, but commitment from the two is required if a much more intimate dance is to be choreographed. In order to do this, partners must come in touch with their deepest yearnings. Motivation deepens when these yearnings are experienced and expressed.

The variety of ways that sculpting can be used is only limited by your creativity and the ground of your experience in experiential design. In addition to sculpting, any form of lively experiment which engages the client by employing forms of experience in addition to verbal dialogue such as space, form, fantasy, movement, play, sound, touch, metaphor will likely increase awareness at both emotional and cognitive levels and augment learning.

When couples begin to take charge, to take authorship of their relational patterns, they become a powerful duo. They will have learned how to work in concert to re-form their relationships, keeping both their individual interests and the welfare of their union equally in mind. The work is difficult but the process, if each is able to persist and weather the chaos, fear, and vulnerability of change, cements the relationship.

Homework is critical when working within managed care as sessions often must be spread apart and the time between sessions must be used to the greatest advantage. Homework in this phase often involves assignments to help develop more harmonious contact and regular, controlled airings of feelings and thoughts using new communication skills and giving equal time to each partner. Often, assignments aimed at increasing emotional awareness and ownership of relationship patterns, including each partner's role in those patterns, are helpful at this stage. Assignments to gather further family data and family lore are also common in this phase. Bibliotherapy can be helpful also.

IDD E ASE TREAT ENT

Therapy is kept lively when the therapist pays attention to whatever current figures (that which stands out and has energy) each partner raises. The therapist can help the couple better formulate these issues and assist the couple in negotiating which issue is of most interest/importance to them as a couple at this time. Relating these present and lively issues to the principle goals which have been identified helps to keep the work focused and unified. Whatever is most present will be more captivating than dusting off old material and trying to resurrect it. However, in counterpoint to this, sometimes focusing the system on an issue which has some urgency but which the couple tends to avoid may be necessary at times. As Satir would coach, attention must continually shift back and forth from what is in foreground to what is in background. Rest assured, the core themes/issues identified earlier will always play out in the present.

During this phase experiments are then constructed to attempt to shift primary dysfunctional dynamics within the couple system, rework unfinished business, alter interactional patterns, shift role behaviors, and forge a new, more satisfying couple system.

Efforts are made in this phase to help the couple to integrate new patterns and healthy rituals and agreements although depending on the length of therapy, new changes will be rooted to varying degrees. Extended family coaching also may be introduced in this phase in order to begin to change dysfunctional patterns with the extended family and/or institute or strengthen functional patterns.

ATE ASE TREAT ENT

The late phase within a managed care context is typically brief. During this time, goals and progress are reviewed and appreciations and disappointments are surfaced and processed. In addition, with the couples' participation, a sound aftercare plan is drawn up. Such a maintenance plan might include tools the couple has learned, agreements to carry on with new rituals, identification of relapse warning signs, link-ups with any community supports that exist for the couple such as couples support groups, church groups, periodic workshops for couples, and periodic check points and check-up criteria.

C NC SI N

Working within the managed care environment is not ideal when working with couples with deeply embedded, multiple, dysfunctional patterns and multiple stressors. Time constraints, except in the most liberal managed care contracts (which are dwindling), do not allow enough time for assessment, building the working relationship, stabilizing the crisis (if the couple enters in that state), developing new awarenesses, attitudes, beliefs, and skills, and integrating changes enough to hold over time. The most that is possible with such couples where plans are quite limited is crisis intervention and stabilization unless they have financial resources to self-pay. While public agencies which offer sliding scale fee schedules have severely dwindled, referring couples in need of further treatment to such agencies or to training centers may be possible.

If one or both partners is (are) characterologically impaired, a special treatment strategy should be employed (Shub, 1994). According to Shub (1994), the best plan in this case is to work individually with the characterologically impaired individual and meet with the couple/family at longer intervals to help facilitate change in the characterologically impaired family member and assist the family in making shifts in dynamics as that family member begins to make change.

Couples in early stages of trouble, couples whose patterns are less embedded or less complicated, couples who have greater inherent strengths and external resources to deal with problematic areas or where stressors are fewer or less severe, fare better within the managed care model. In addition, more highly trained therapists can more effectively and efficiently intervene. Advanced training for therapists is now even more imperative. Focused goals which cut to the quick of the most serious problems, use of psychoeducational programs, spacing sessions two or three weeks apart if possible, and assigning and following up on homework all have the potential of advancing the therapy process.

Conceptualizing the therapy process in units of work, prioritzing those units, focusing on one unit at a time, and using the revolving door to complete all units over a longer time frame is a viable option. Some clients may have the resources to continue therapy as a self-pay client if reeducated in that direction at the outset.

Multi-generational approaches are clearly here to stay. If we implement our theories with acumen, we can fare well in the managed care arena. At least for now, I believe this is true. However, what would enhance recognition of this approach as viable would be well-designed outcome research. As it stands now, the medical community and managed care community favor cognitive-behavioral approaches simply because this approach has the largest base of empirical research supporting its efficacy.

Some large managed care companies are now insisting that therapists on their panels achieve a high level of competency in cognitive-behavioral therapy because research on this approach has consistently shown it to be effective. If we fail to support rigorous research to demonstrate the efficacy of other approaches, managed care may in the near future attempt to dictate the theoretical approaches we embrace if we are to remain in their good standing. If this happens we are in part responsible. Serious outcome research may forestall this eventuality.

REFERENCES

Carter, . and Mc oldrick, M. (1988). *The changing family life cycle* (2nd Edition). New ork: ardner Press.

erson, ., Hoffman, S., Sauls, M., Ulrici, D. (1993). Family of origin frames in couples therapy. *Journal of Marriage and amily Therapy,* 19, ( ), 3 1-3 .

erson, . and Mc oldrick, M. (1986). Constructing and interpreting genograms: the example of Sigmund Freud s family. In P.A. eller and . . itt (Eds.), *Innovations in Clinical Practice: A Source Book: ol. 5* (pp. 203-219). Sarasota F : Pro esource.

erson, . (198). Systems psychotherapy, the micro-computer, and the American Family. *Marriage and amily Review,* 8, (1-2), 1 -16 .

Mc oldrick, M. and erson, . (198). *Genograms in amily Assessment.* N. .: W.W. Norton.

Nevis, E. (1997). estalt therapy and organi ational development: A historical perspective. *Gestalt Review,* 1, (2), 110-130.

ohrbaugh, M., ogers, J.C., and Mc oldrick, M. (1992). How do experts read family genograms *amily Systems Medicine,* 10, (1), 79-89.

Satir, V. and anmen, J., erber, J., amori, M. (1991). *The Satir Model.* Palo Alto, California: Science and ehavior ooks, Inc.

Shub, N. (199). The Process of Character Work: An Introduction, *orking Paper Series.* Columbus, Ohio: estalt Associates.

Therapy with Men in Relationships in a Managed Care Environment

Robert A. Barcus

SUMMARY. Managed care affects all facets of psychotherapy practice. This article discusses the specific problems associated with working with men in couples therapy under managed care. ased on the clinical e pe- rience of the author, managed care contributes to difficulties in the fol- lowing areas fle ibility of treatment, access to treatment, administrative burdens for the therapist, limits on the choice of therapeutic modality, and ade uate reimbursement. *[Article copies availa le for a fee from The Haworth Document Delivery Service: 8 34 678. E mail address: getinfo haworthpressinc.com e site: http: www.haworthpressinc.com*

KEYWORDS. Managed care, men, relationships, couples, therapy

Engaging male partners in psychotherapy is traditionally a difficult task. Men are reluctant, resistant, and guarded (Levant, 199 ; Wilcox Forrest, 1992). They often come to therapy only under threat of sepa- ration or divorce or if otherwise persuaded by their spouse or partner (Shay, 1996). They may need encouragement and sensitive handling

---

obert A. arcus is a clinical psychologist and Clinical Director of the ellow Springs Psychological Center, a private practice group. He is also on the clinical faculty at Wright State University in the School of Professional Psychology and the School of Medicine, Department of Psychiatry.

Address correspondence to: obert A. arcus, PhD, Clinical Director, ellow Springs Psychological Center, 213 enia Avenue, ellow Springs, OH 387.

[Haworth co-indexing entry note]: "Therapy with Men in altionships in a Managed Care nviron- ment." Barcus, obert A. Co-published simultaneously in *Journal of Couples Therapy* (The Haworth Press, Inc.) Vol. 8, No. 3/4, 1999, pp. 5-34; and: *Couples Therapy in Managed Care: Facing the Crisis* (ed: Barbara Jo Brothers) The Haworth Press, Inc., 1999, pp. 5-34. Single or multiple copies of this article are available for a fee from The Haworth ocument elivery Service [1-8 -34 -9 8, 9: a.m. - 5: p.m. (ST). -mail address: getinfo haworthpressinc.com].

until they are really committed to the process. Once fully involved, however, men can make dramatic changes that positively affect their mental and physical health and their relationships with their partners and families (Allen   Gordon, 199 ; Barcus, 1997).

Working with men in couples therapy under optimal conditions requires a therapist to be aware of men's issues including their discomfort with being one-down in a hierarchical relationship, men's difficulty in expressing and empathizing with affect, their propensity to intellectualize and minimize difficulties, and their desire for a quick fix (Levant, 1996; Meth   Pasick, 199). Attempting this work under a managed care environment poses additional encumbrances in the following areas: flexibility, access, administrative burden, therapeutic modality, and reimbursement.

In the last decade all psychotherapists have been forced to adapt to the new reality that therapy will be scrutinized and regulated by an entity with the dual mandate of providing health care while minimizing costs and maximizing their profit (Economist, 1998; Strupp, 1997). The inherent conflict in these roles has created a challenging tension for therapist navigating between the client and payor.

In this article I will share learnings from my own clinical experience in private practice with a large number of men in couples therapy and with a wide variety of managed care organizations (MCOs), preferred provider organizations (PPOs), and health maintenance organizations (HMOs). I will refer to these various third party payor systems generally as MCOs unless a distinction needs to be drawn. And while not all systems or individual case managers operate similarly, some generalizations can be made.

Likewise, male clients vary, presenting a wide range of challenges and rewards; but again, some generalizations will be attempted. I will be focusing on men in couples therapy although many elements will apply to other modalities of therapy as well. I realize a couple may be married or not, gay or heterosexual, but I will often use the term spouse, wife, or partner interchangeably since the majority of couples presenting for therapy are married men and women.

E I I IT AND ACCESS

It is frequently difficult getting men into therapy in the first place (Good, Dell,   Mintz, 1989). Many come only following an ultimatum from their wives (Gordon   Allen, 199). The couple is then faced with the challenge of finding an appropriate therapist who has both the expertise and the personal qualities to relate to the couple. We know that the relationship fit leading to a strong therapeutic alliance is one of the most important nonspecific variables in potentiating successful therapy outcome (Krupnick et al., 1996; Lambert   Okiishi, 1997; Whiston   Sexton, 1993).   nder some managed care systems a new male client would have to go to an HMO facility where he would be assigned a therapist, often inexperienced and perhaps without the skills to overcome the many obstacles to successful couples therapy.

Since men have particular problems in a hierarchical relationship where they are in a one down position, being with a younger therapist is particularly problematic. In other cases, due to limits on the PPOs panel membership, the male client might not be able to be referred to the best available therapist or a therapist who was personally recommended by a trusted friend or physician. I have had many men come to me following unsuccessful experiences in couples therapy with a therapist not attuned to men's issues. Many of these men were turned off to therapy for some time following an experience where they only felt blamed or felt that they needed somehow to feminize their personal style. Others felt that they and their spouse were hastily analyzed and given a prescriptive approach to change without the therapeutic support to implement such changes. Some men will give therapy a shot–but only one. And if it's a disastrous experience it will harden their resistance to further work. It is a shame for couples not to be able to access a therapist who has been recommended and thus more likely to be trusted or one with real relevant experience when the relationship is on the line.

Often men are invited to join therapy with their wives or partners after the women are engaged in individual work themselves. In a managed care environment it may be difficult to flexibly include a spouse in ongoing individual therapy due to the nature of an already approved treatment plan for the wife. Further, in some cases once the man has been initially engaged in couples therapy, he may be willing to be referred for additional individual therapy to support the couples work. Ideally, this would be with a therapist with a good collegial relationship with the couple's therapist so that easy collaboration would be possible. However, there may be limitations imposed on the choice of that therapist. For example, in our practice we often like to have an individual therapist for each member of the couple and then collaborate in conjoint therapy. Being in the same practice, with regular clinical meetings and having excellent working relationships, makes this kind of clinical collaboration very productive for the client and efficient for us. Alternatively, the client may work with a therapist with whom we have a long-standing professional association which engenders an atmosphere of trust and cooperation among all parties. nfortunately, MCO restrictions often disable this effective option.

Recent articles in the professional literature and public press have decried the problems concerning the lack of confidentiality of health insurance information (Davidson, I.   Davidson, T., 1996; Davidson, T.   Davidson, J., 1995). Once information is sent to an MCO, the clinician no longer retains control over it. This information may be held in electronic data systems and be accessible to unknown others. It is widely known that insurance companies share much information about the health care utilization of individuals through a large data clearinghouse. Many men are particularly sensitive to such issues because they fear that their careers may be jeopardized if their employers know they are having "problems." Since it is usually the employer who is providing and paying for the insurance, employees feel especially vulnerable. This is particularly critical to men in, or working for, the military or in government positions where they may deal with sensitive or security information. Male members of disturbed relationships have been reluctant to be identified as a "patient" and have personal information sent to some case manager. Some of these men choose to pay for their psychotherapy out of pocket if they can afford it. In some cases the therapy work can proceed as long as the female partner is the identified patient, but other men opt out of the therapy altogether.

I work near a large Air Force base with a substantial technical and research component. It is tragic when men allow their primary relationships to suffer because of the perceived career risk of being seen as emotionally unstable. I have seen men who have avoided needed therapy for years because of their fears and have finally assented to therapy only in the face of an overwhelming crisis. Ironically, the exacerbated family and marital problems work against not only the men, but the Air Force mission as well as these men in crisis at home frequently report that their occupational function diminishes significantly.

For gay couples, having a therapist write a treatment plan recognizing their homosexual relationship difficulties raises the specter of divulging their sexual orientation to a system whose ability to protect privacy is suspect. For some men this is a serious problem and an impediment to therapy. Writing a treatment plan to address the underlying psychological issues without mentioning the sexual orientation of the client is possible sometimes, but at other times is merely an exercise in obfuscation.

Flexible case management can be a real plus in dealing with an anxious and skeptical male client who is tentatively exploring therapy. However, under managed care it can be cumbersome to flexibly move back and forth between couples and individual work as needed, having to rewrite treatment plans or reconceptualize each decision for some third party. Further, since many men benefit from men's group therapy it may be difficult to move between the couples work and group work for the same reasons. Each change in modality can require tedious phone calls and conferences with the hard-to-reach case manager or extensive treatment plans with justifications for clinical judgment.

T ERA E TIC   DA IT

Following managed care's imperative for brief therapy will mean that men get only limited, shallow therapy, focusing on cognitive issues and solutions to observable problems. While this may produce some benefits and bring some immediate relief, what men may need, and what wives are so often yearning for, is for men to make fundamental character shifts and be enabled to make more emotional and intimate contact with them (Johnson, 1997). The kinds of concerns that are contributing to the enormous divorce rate are, in my experience, about deep, existential, and humanistic issues. Developing empathy and understanding, intimate sharing abilities, and a sense of family inclusion requires significant learning about oneself and how to communicate and be in a relationship with another (Walker, Johnson, Manion, Cloutier, 1996; inker, 1994). Such therapy does not translate well into the typical MCO treatment plan.

Paradoxically, men may in fact be more comfortable initially with the kind of therapy promoted by MCOs: brief, cognitive, programmatic, and problem focused. However, with time a skilled therapist can open them up to the value of deeper work. It is common for couples to experience significant relief just by coming to therapy and, in a safe and supportive environment, being able to share their concerns. With the therapist to help prevent the usual bitter arguments and hurt feelings, couples generally appreciate the opportunity to share and be heard. Many times the men, especially, are quite willing to terminate therapy after only a few sessions with the impasse temporarily overcome (Kupers, 1993). However, under such circumstances little new behavior has been integrated and the crisis has merely ebbed. Within a short period of time the partners are back where they started, and then they are feeling that even therapy is hopeless because they have tried that. This may spell doom for the relationship.

It would be far more productive for the couple–and beneficial for society–for these couples to be permitted the impactful, longer term psychotherapy necessary to facilitate significant and lasting change. If we encourage men to terminate following brief problem-solving interventions, couples will fail to gain the longer term advantage of meaningful psychotherapy.

The kind of therapy that saves couples may not conform to the managed care paradigm. Many men come for therapy impelled by a demand from their wives for more affective awareness, sharing, and the ability to form a more intimate relationship. However, these kinds of problems, even though they may threaten to rend a family, causing separation, divorce, depression and other serious mental disorders, do not fit neatly into a treatment plan. Telling an MCO case manager about a therapeutic goal of preventing serious problems from impacting a family, by teaching a male to be more aware of his feelings and to participate in an intimate relationship, will perhaps earn a word of appreciation but no authorized sessions.

Preventative work of all kinds is difficult for a therapist to justify to an MCO. This poses a particular problem in practicing men's health psychology. For example, I have never had a problem getting authorizations for working with men *a ter* their heart attack. But it is difficult to write an acceptable treatment plan for lifestyle change to alter coronary-prone behavior *e ore* an incident. The impact on the marriage and family of such an event can be enormous. Men face many health risks (Vogele, Jarvis, Cheeseman, 1997) and die at an earlier age than women (Kranczer, 1997). A great proportion of these risks are voluntary behaviors such as drinking, smoking, diet or other patterns that are within men's ability to change, such as learning to relieve stress with healthy social relationships, taking time for relaxation, or exercise. Yet there is little opportunity, in spite of the mission of

HMOs, to treat the health behaviors of men in couples *e ore* a serious physical ailment strikes.

REI RSE ENT

In addition to the decline of fees for psychotherapy across the board there are special reimbursement problems related with working with men in couples. For example, in our practice we have had significant success helping men learn to be more sensitive in their relationships with partners through participating in men's therapy groups. When it is intimacy that must be taught, there is no better venue than a group, with its network of intimate relationships. Men respond well to the modeling of other men who are struggling with similar issues. MCOs have been generally supportive of group therapy because of the lower cost per client. However, they keep pushing the reimbursement levels lower. For example, we run our groups for two hours to allow men adequate time to warm up, overcome their natural resistance, and get some real work done. We do this despite knowing that no third party payer will reimburse us for more than one-and-a-half hours. We are willing to take some loss to provide what we believe is quality therapy. However, one large MCO is now paying only 22 for group therapy. After paying my overhead and splitting the balance with a co-therapist, I'm earning less than minimum wage for treating that client. If the financial base of group therapy continues to be eroded, this valuable intervention may become unavailable.

An endemic problem in doing all kinds of couples therapy is the need to have one of the partners diagnosed with a DSM IV Axis I disorder in order to be reimbursed by insurance. Partner Relational Problem is a V code and not reimbursable which forces the therapist to diagnose an individual disorder. While some men may be willing to participate in "couples therapy" many of them are loathe to be identified with a "mental disorder." At times this resistance can be overcome, but at other times, men have chosen instead to refrain from therapy.

AD INISTRATI E RDEN

All through this discussion we see the need to write treatment plans, contact case managers, and proceed in a prescribed manner. This is endemic to all work with MCOs. It may be slightly exacerbated with men in couples relationships because by its nature such therapy may require flexible and changing modalities: individual, couples, or group therapy. And men may be more sensitive about being diagnosed and having confidential information shared with an MCO.

Each change demands more time spent communicating with the third party payor or its agent. Such time is unreimbursable and given the Byzantine nature of some treatment plans and the difficulty contacting case managers for telephone reviews, this time can be considerable. These burdens may discourage some therapists from being willing to provide couples treatment.

C NC SI N

These factors make it more difficult to provide psychotherapy for men in relationships. Therapists are caught between the devil and the deep blue sea: we can either eschew managed care and risk the failure of our ability to practice at all or we can cooperate with it and risk our ability to practice as we see fit. Having chosen to attempt the latter–to accommodate to the current health care realities–I believe that in order to survive as a therapist it is imperative to understand the priorities and requirements of MCOs.

My personal experience is that careful attention to the treatment plan and using high professional standards and a solid theoretical analysis of the proposed therapy gives the case manager the rationale for my proposed treatment and thus the support to authorize. Case managers also have to answer to their supervisors and we assist them by writing an adequate treatment plan that fits within their guidelines and justifies the authorization. I have found that doing so in most cases results in a favorable determination and the support of the MCO although there are occasionally puzzling responses and apparently arbitrary rigidities. Establishing and maintaining a good working relationship with individual case managers can also help although their high rate of turnover makes this a daunting task. Calling and negotiating exceptions to the standard procedure is possible and can create the necessary flexibility. However, all of this does significantly increase the therapist's unreimbursed workload in an environment of decreasing fees.

The shattering of intimate social relationships extracts a toll on individuals and society. Productive work time is lost, self care and personal health diminishes, and costs are increased when significant relationships fail. In addition, family alliances are broken, emotional support decreases, and children sadly suffer. While the managed care revolution has brought previously escalating health care costs under control, it has also created new problems. Hopefully, thoughtful discussion of these issues can lead to the realization that providing adequate and accessible psychotherapy that is appropriate to the client will benefit the insurer and MCO, the client, and society.

REFERENCES

Allen, J. A.   ordon, S. (1990). Creating a framework for change. In   . . Meth
 . S. Pasick (Eds.), *Men in therapy: The challenge of change* (pp. 131-1 1). New
 ork: Plenum.
  arcus,   . (1997). Partners of survivors of abuse: A men s therapy group. *Psycho
 therapy, 34* 316-323.
Davidson, J.   .   Davidson, T. (1996). Confidentiality and managed care: Ethical
 and legal concerns. *Health   Social   ork,   , 208-21 .
Davidson, T.   Davidson, J.   . (199). Cost containment, computers, and confidentiality. *Clinical Social   ork Journal, 3,   3- 6 .
Economist (1998). Health care in America. *The Economist, 346* (80 8), 23-26.
  ood,   . E., Dell, D. M.,   Mint ,   . . (1989). Male role and gender role conflict:
  elations to help-seeking in men. *Journal of Counseling Psychology, 36,*
 29 -300.
  ordon,   .,   Allen, J. A. (1990). Helping men in couple relationships. In   . .
 Meth   . S. Pasick (Eds.), *Men in therapy: The challenge of change* (pp. 181-
 208). New   ork: Plenum.
Johnson, S. M. (1997). Predictors of success in emotionally focused marital therapy.
 Journal of Marital and   amily Therapy, 3, 13 -1 2.
  ranc er, S. (1997).   ecord high U. S. life expectancy. *Statistical Bulletin Metropol
 itan Insurance Companies, 78* ( ), 2-8.
  rupnick, J.   ., Sotsky, S. M., Simmens, S., Moyer, J., Elkin, I., Watkins, J.,
 Pilkonis, P.A. (1996). The role of the therapeutic alliance in psychotherapy and
 pharmacotherapy outcome: Findings in the National Institute of Mental Health
 treatment of depression collaborative research program. *Journal of Consulting
 and Clinical Psychology, 64,*   32- 39.
  upers, T. A. (1993). *Revisioning men's lives: Gender intimacy and power.* New
 ork: uilford.
  ambert, M. J.   Okiishi, J. C. (1997). The effects of the individual psychotherapist
 and implications for future research. *Clinical Psychology: Science and Practice,
 4,* 66-7 .
  evant,   . F. (1990). Psychological Services designed for men: A psychoeducational
 approach. *Psychotherapy, 7,* 309-31

evant, . F. (1996). The new psychology of men. *Professional Psychology: Re search and Practice, 7, 2* 9-26 .

Meth, . . Pasick, . S. (1990). *Men in therapy: The challenge of change.* New ork: uilford.

Shay, J. J. (1996). Okay, I m here, but I m not talking Psychotherapy with the reluctant male. *Psychotherapy, 33,* 03- 13.

Strupp, H. H. (1997). esearch, practice, and managed care. *Psychotherapy, 34,* 91-9 .

Vogele, C., Jarvis, A., Cheeseman, . (1997). Anger suppression, reactivity, and hypertension risk: ender makes a difference. *Annals of Behavioral Medicine,* , 61-69.

Walker, J. ., Johnson, S., Manion, I., Cloutier, P. (1996). Emotionally focused marital intervention for couples with chronically ill children. *Journal of Consult ing and Clinical Psychology, 64,* 1029-1036.

Whiston, S. C., Sexton, T. I. (1993). An overview of psychotherapy outcome research: Implications for practice. *Professional Psychology: Research and Prac tice, 4,* 3- 1.

Wilcox, D. W., Forrest, . (1992). The problems of men and counseling: ender bias or gender truth *Journal of Mental Health Counseling, 4,* 291-30 .

inker, J. C. (199). *In search of good form: Gestalt therapy with couples and families.* New ork: Jossey- ass.

Working with Couples
in the Current Environment

Judith R. Brown

SUMMARY. ouples and families as units of treatment emerged as a ma or shift from the medical model prevalent up until about forty years ago. o longer was an individual spouse or child singled out and labelled as patient rather, family interaction became the focus for the early pioneers of family therapy. ow managed care influences decisions formerly made by marriage and family practitioners whom we treat, diagnoses, length of treatment, methodology, even the education necessary for licensure. e need to keep the human element and practical knowledge in our profession and realize the limits of trying to be more "scientific." *Article copies availa le for a fee from The Haworth Document Delivery Service: 8 34 678. E mail address: getinfo haworthpressinc. com e site: http: www.haworthpressinc.com*

KEYWORDS. Managed care, couples, relational view, medicalization, humanness

The field of couples therapy is always in a state of flux with its continual development and expansion of various approaches to practice, its interrelations with other psychotherapies, and its actions and reactions to state and federal legal systems. What currently gives a new cast to these ongoing influences and complexities is the dark

---

Judith . rown, PhD, is President of eorge and Judith rown, International Consultants.

[Haworth co-indexing entry note]: "Wor ing with Couples in the Current nvironment." Brown, Judith . Co-published simultaneously in *Journal of Couples Therapy* (The Haworth Press, Inc.) Vol. 8, No. 3/4, 1999, pp. 35-55; and: *Couples Therapy in Managed Care: Facing the Crisis* (ed: Barbara Jo Brothers) The Haworth Press, Inc., 1999, pp. 35-55. Single or multiple copies of this article are available for a fee from The Haworth ocument elivery Service [1-8 -34 -9 8, 9: a.m. - 5: p.m. (ST). -mail address: getinfo haworthpressinc.com].

shadow of managed care. Central to this discussion are thoughts about the current path of the marriage and family therapy (MFT) profession, the extent to which the big business of health care dominates what we study, whom we see, how we work and the direction in which we are headed. Most important to consider is whether the relationship between therapist and clients is suffering under the changes that are occurring. What will become of the human aspects that are particularly central to our profession: the interpersonal emphases such as trust, contact, practical knowledge and inspiration?

A   E ER A TER

For me folktales and couples' therapy have certain similarities: the repetition of behavior, common themes, and always the realization that this tale or this family is unique. The frequent retelling of stories with their engaging details and universal subject matter are perennial, as are the rhythm of the sentences and familiar phrases: the "fe, fi, fo fum" of the ogre in Jack and the Beanstalk; "I ran away from the little old woman and the little old man, and I can run away from you, I can I can" in The Gingerbread Man. Surely I am not the only one who has met the ogre (as well as his sabotaging wife) and the Gingerbread Man in my practice. As youngsters we learn that in fiction something always happens to make a story worth telling. In real life marriage and couples therapy we trust that we can help to cause bring about something different, a new narrative with something new and exciting happening. Like children hearing folktales, we may believe that the good guys, and even we ourselves, might live happily ever after.

The current environment does not bode well for the happy ever after outcome. It is not an easy time for couples. To put our present situation into perspective, couples in all eras, I suppose, have discovered that the honeymoon trip–even for princes and princesses–is just the beginning, and the course of marriage can be quite another adventure. The people we see today are lucky if they can coordinate their crammed schedules to plan a wedding and arrange child-care for a honeymoon! Time pressures[1] create a juggling act out of every day, and one cannot afford to drop either work, child-care, doctors' appointments, or chauffeuring children or older parents to classes and appointments. All must be kept moving in perfect coordination. Add to such requirements of today's frantic life the widespread financial difficulties, the profusion and confusion of step families, and the usual time consuming and perpetual necessities of family maintenance; and to top it all off, the expectations of intimacy, equality, good communication and satisfying sex. We are looking at overtaxed systems.

As for us, the therapists of these couples and families; dare we hope for happy ever after? We have our own pressures–relationship and otherwise. Following a day of coping with couples, clinics and hospitals, child protective services, and the mountains of paperwork that seem to grow at an exponential rate, happy ever after is far beyond the simple survival of which we dream. We also have journals and newsletters to read and continuing education credits to accumulate. For we are professionals who are expected not only to keep up with new developments in our areas of expertise but to expand these areas. We are constantly reminded of such expectations by the partially-read journals that sit silently piled up on desk and book shelf. Latest approaches are proclaimed in new vocabularies, fresh hope for mastery and success, followed by articles further explicating the theories, building on the original ideas, and advertisements for training seminars and workshops to teach all. Like couples' relationships, each approach is unique in some way. And like folktales, each contributes in its own way. We never can keep up with the reading! nlike folktales that take place "once upon a time," our profession is ongoing through time; we do not come to the end of the story, nor can we predict what changes in the larger community will influence how we practice next month or next year, or indeed, if we still practice at all.

E   E   R   N

Marriage and family therapy is part of a larger field of psychotherapy which it influences and by which it is influenced. There have been major changes in the profession in the last four decades: in sheer numbers of practitioners, in the political realm of legalities governing training, interaction with the community and clients, and in theory and practice. Thirty years ago when my husband applied for his MFC license in California, he had only to submit three letters attesting to his moral character and ability to work with people, along with proof of an advanced degree in a related field (broadly interpreted). No exam, written or oral, no internship, no supervised hours–none of these were required. His license number is 2265. Now in California there are

23,31   currently licensed MFTs. Our state organization, California
Association of Marriage and Family Therapists (CAMFT), has a legal
counsel who observes and becomes involved in the workings of the
state government; he provides information in our journal about new
legislation which affects us and our clients, directly or indirectly.

> We generally sponsor between three to five bills a year.
> CAMFT's legislative agenda for this two-year session is both
> varied and bold. We are now in the process of finding authors for
> the six bills that we intend to sponsor this year. The topics vary
> from managed care (continuity of care), to licensing board disci-
> plinary actions, to signing certifications for involuntary commit-
> ments, to expanding permissible work settings for interns and
> trainees . . . (Leslie, 1997, p. 6)

The counsel reminds his readers that we, the members of local
chapters of the state organization, are needed to help "garner support
from our state Assemblypersons and Senators. . . . since we can
expect major battles." So in this larger field of state politics, we and
our clients are directly affected by legislation introduced at the instiga-
tion of our organization, as well as issues affecting our profession to a
greater or lesser degree, such as contributions by political action com-
mittees (PACs) to candidates for office. The many local and state
organizations throughout the country and the national organization
(American Association of Marriage and Family Therapists, AAMFT)
work to lead the profession for our benefit and for our clients. As
practitioners our voices may be heard through the local and state
organs through which we receive information via newsletters and
journals.

T E RE ATI NA   IE

Intrinsic to the early development of couples and family therapy
was the removal of the patient label from an individual spouse or child
and to focus on the interaction between the couple or among the
members of the family. "Individual ownership of the problem is thus
shifted to relational patterns. The problem is moved from *insi e* individual family members to the transactions *among* family members"
(Minuchin, 1996, p. 71). It is easy to forget what a major shift this was

from the general outlook of psychology and psychiatry. Sullivan's book, *nterpersonal Theory o sy hiatry* (1953), was a precursor to Satir, Bateson, Bowen, Haley, Minuchin, Whitaker and other giants on whose shoulders our profession has been built. In a clear departure from the medical model that focused on individual psychopathology and treatment, we have stood for systems thinking about pathology and family dynamics for forty years.

Family therapy is grounded in the idea of paying close attention to the couple or family in action. Therein lies the possibility to facilitate changes for healthier functioning of the system and growth in all individuals members. This shift from the medical model of a single identified patient was not universally espoused. Like many new ideas, it was rejected by those who saw it as conflicting and competing with their own accepted practice. Large numbers in the mainstream of the profession have continued to perceive one member of a family system as ill and in need of cure–be it a psychological approach or a drug, or both–rather than to consider the system-as-client in need of treatment. These two paradigms, the medical and the systemic approaches to treatment, are still evident in the ways problems in the family are approached. I quote from a letter, one of many printed in Family *Therapy ews*, prompted by the death of Harry Goolishian. "He was one of the early developers of family therapy who helped family therapy escape from the medical model" (Vol. 23, Number 1, Feb. 1992, p. 19). This gives an indication of the feelings of many who saw, and still see, family therapy as having to break free from the approach of individual diagnosis and treatment, ignoring the larger family system.

A SE ARATE IDENTIT

MFTs are newcomers in the psychotherapy arena, and appear to be at the bottom of this totem pole in the hierarchy of status. Psychiatry, a branch of medicine, claims top position, reflecting the high regard for science and medical degrees in our culture. MFTs see clients with emotional problems of every degree of severity. Couples and families call upon us to help deal with relationship conflicts, that is, all manner of problems of living and dying. In my memory we were MFCCs, that is, marriage, family and child counselors. I suppose that a "therapist" is seen as higher status than a "counselor." Having children, couples and families as clients is demanding in the extreme, requiring a combination of art and science and a keen ability to observe people and their interactions, to tolerate and deal with highly emotional situations, and use ourselves creatively in the process.

R   ESSI NA IS

It is only a matter of time before all states require an MFT license. California, the state I am most familiar with, has had an active state organization for many years, creating and fostering a climate for growth and development of the profession. This is evidenced by the advent (decades ago) of an examination for licensure that gave rise to special courses to help prepare people in weekends of cramming. Specific major areas of study in institutions for "marriage and family" followed, and finally schools specializing entirely in family studies. The licensing exams changed over the years, reflecting changing emphases in practice and the broader scope of knowledge considered relevant. As a component of their preparation, would-be marriage/family therapists are obliged to gain experience working with various populations in assorted settings. A critical new requirement heralding an official shift in outlook has been added: knowledge of the standard book of guidelines for diagnosing mental disorders, the DSM, put out by the American Psychiatric Association.

"DSM" stands for *iagnosti an   tatisti al Man al o Mental isor ers.* "It has largely become the common language of behavioral health which its authors intended, used for research, teaching, and clinical practice" (Denton, Patterson, Van Meir, 1997, p. 81). "The Commission on Accreditation for Marriage and Family Education (COAMFTE, 1991), mandates that 'students will learn to diagnose and treat . . . nervous and mental disorders, whether cognitive, affective, or behavioral (p. 14)' " (Denton et al., 1997, p. 81). It is suggested that some confusion exists about this requirement for MFTs, that some "training directors expressed the perception that not only is instruction in the DSM not required but that it is actually discouraged by the COAMFTE (despite what the COAMFTE standards state) (M. A. Armour, personal communication, November, 1993)" (Denton et al., p. 83). Results of the survey the authors conducted showed:

> nearly all of the responding marriage and family therapy programs are teaching their students the use of the DSM . . . It

appears that the motivation for teaching the DSM is primarily pragmatic and does not signify a paradigmatic shift in the field of marriage and family. Interdisciplinary communication, improved chances of employment, and cooperation with third-party payers were the main reasons cited for teaching in this area. Few positive comments (and many negative) about the DSM were made, even by those programs teaching it.

In the first paragraph of the "Cautionary Statement" page xxvii of the manual (1994), it states that guidelines are necessary, "because it has been demonstrated that the use of such criteria enhances agreement among clinicians and investigators. The proper use of these criteria requires specialized clinical training that provides both a body of knowledge and clinical skills."

C NSE   ENCES   EDICA I ATI N

The authors of the survey remark that it does not seem to represent a "paradigmatic shift." Embracing the DSM seems to represent, if not a categorical turning away from the emphasis of a systemic view, a definite shove in that direction. Granted there have been signs along the way of such a shift. However, this latest imperative, in combination with HMO requirements, goes much further. It creates the necessity for one or both people in a couple, or a single member of a family, to be dealt an individual diagnosis. I wonder what the influence of teaching the DSM in marriage/family training is on practitioners now and what it indicates for the future. Does this affect how we deal with our couples and families; if so, in what respects?

Managed care may be the most recent and far-reaching of current issues affecting our profession. The words themselves managed care– imply a benevolent, parental presence. Despite its euphony, for many it has come to symbolize a rapidly growing creature out of a science fiction horror movie; a massive octopus whose powerful, greedy arms reach out and threaten devastation. How did this beast come to be among us, touching so many in negative ways? Who let this creation into our midst? It was accepted through mistrust of government and the gullibility of the population desperate for a health system that would solve the problems of inordinate medical costs.   nder this new system, we have, according to Larry Amsel, M.D.:

fewer insured, less choice, less access to hospital care, less access to specialists, less mental health benefits, major interference in the doctor-patient relationship, denials of appeals when services are cut off, less confidentiality of our medical records, less care for the poor, less medical education, less research, less accountability, and higher real costs for Medicare. What we don't have are any of the benefits we were promised. (p. 25, *Tikk n*, May/June, 1997)

In their article, "Forging a New Trail: Emerging Trends for MFTs," Conley and Miles (1997) present the many complexities that currently bear upon our profession, including the proliferation of HMOs and the potential conflict they present.

The insurance/managed care model is dependent on pathology to justify treatment. Since the true value of marriage and family counseling is in helping people recognize and develop new skills in relating rather than defining or fixing pathology, there is an inherent conflict between much of what MFCCs (sic) are licensed to do and the present health benefits system. Many therapists will recognize the ethical dilemma of determining a pathology-based (i.e., DSM) diagnosis in order to support clients who request third-party reimbursement. (*The   ali ornia Therapist*, Vol. 9, Jan./Feb., p. 49)

The development of marriage and family therapy as a distinct profession has led, paradoxically, to some blurring of distinctions between us and other professions dealing with mental disorders. The increasing numbers of people pursuing MFT licensure face barriers of more intense courses of study, more hours of supervised training, demanding internships, and increasingly tough examinations. Now that the scope of clients we are trained to work with increases, new laws define where and how we fit into the larger health care systems and insurance payments. As a result of the inevitable overlaps with other mental health providers, some practitioners are deprived of their former professional domain. Others, like MFTs, are faced with new opportunities. The way is paved in some states for MFTs to move into medical arenas where they may be in positions of making recommendations about the necessity for hospitalization of clients, and to work in concert with medical doctors and psychiatric nurses, and on special wards in hospitals.

Other consequences of the development of our profession may be more subtle but equally powerful; these stem from the importance of the words and metaphors we use when we speak of clients and treatment.

> The way we define and talk about our work has a lot to do with how we do therapy. If we think medically in order to fill out a treatment plan for the HMO, for example, that will influence how we do the therapy, even . . . if we don't want it to. Far more pervasive, however, is the influence the medical metaphor has in training situations, when students, who are highly anxious to perform well as beginning therapists, imbibe the medical metaphor and "treat" clients on that basis. The student's internal data base is founded, then, on medical thinking. (Feldhaus 1997)

What factors have motivated this trend of MFTs, or the organizations that represent us, to join the track of more medically oriented health care professionals? Surely it is a way to compete for insurance and HMO coverage. Might it also be an attempt to prove our legitimacy, to consider ourselves as *tr e* professionals in our own eyes and the eyes of others, to become more like psychologists, who become more like psychiatrists? Are we wanting to climb closer to the status of doctors by being more scientific? I think it significant that in the index of *oget s Thesa r s* (Authorized American Edition, 1933), the word "scientific" has one synonym following it: "exact" (p. 629). In the physical (hard) sciences, exactness and objectivity have been important concepts, exemplified by the use of quantitative and statistical methodologies in research. In the social sciences a determined effort has been made to emulate the practices and methodologies of exactness and objectivity. Only in the last few decades, especially in the most recent years, qualitative methodologies are becoming acceptable for research studies in the social sciences (Brown, 1996). This development follows the realization that some knowledge can be discovered best, or only by means of research which would "capture the complexity and creativity of meaningful human activity . . . " (Wiener 199).

To go further with the issue of the medicalization of MFTs, I turn to a friend, Marco de Vries, a medical doctor, who was for the major part of his career a professor of pathology at Erasmus Medical School in Rotterdam. Near the end of his career he established The Helen Dowling Institute for Biopsychosocial Medicine. Recently he wrote:

> A month ago–during a supervision–I asked therapists to write down everything they know about their client, how she/he should change and what they (the therapists) should do to make them change. Some of them told me next supervision how this writing down had set them free, so they could really sit with the client and see, feel, and listen and respond. Then new, fresh and unexpected experiences followed. The essence of science is driven by curiosity, wonder and engagement in this wonderful world. What keeps us back is fear of *not knowing* and its corollary, loss of control. (personal communication, March, 1997)

A IN S ACE   R T E ART

Psychiatric diagnoses and theories may help us to feel more in control. Perhaps they help create the illusion of coming from a place of knowing, of knowing how our clients should change, knowing what and how we as therapists should do to "make" these changes in our clients. On the other hand, to "see, feel, listen and respond," to allow–even encourage–"new, fresh and unexpected experiences," seems to leave ourselves open and vulnerable, uncertain about what may happen in this relationship we have with our clients, and not so comfortably in control.

This fear is clearly expressed by a young, inexperienced supervisee of Salvador Minuchin in *Mastering Family Therapy* (Minuchin, 1996, Chapter 7). The wife in the case "had received a spectrum of psychiatric labels over her quarter century of patienthood: chronic schizophrenia, organic mood disorder, multiple substance abuse, and paranoid schizophrenia." The husband was alcoholic; a tough case by anyone's standards. The therapist, Margaret, opted to leave the fourteen year-old daughter out of the sessions to "limit my sense of being overwhelmed." Subsequently she writes, "My fear is not that I'll lose control of the session, but that she (the wife) will go crazy. She gets a symptom. I get scared of this." At one point Minuchin says to her: "She scares you, but she also angers you." Scared and angry! We might all prefer to avoid these feelings, especially when in the role of therapist. Yet how many opportunities for contact and change we miss when we restrict the new, fresh and unexpected thing from happening. Margaret gets the message that she needs to grow past her fear. And so must we all. It is our humanness that may hold us back; yet it is our humanness, above all, through which we can practice our art, make meaningful connections and facilitate the growth of our clients.

T E RIES AND C T RA ICTI N

A "scientific" path may give one a false impression of having some control of a situation. Being well-versed in theory and psychiatric diagnostic criteria are ways of becoming familiar with abstractions of others' reasoning, with partial descriptions of others' observations. These formulations and speculations can, like theories, be useful in helping to map the territory; just as a map in the pocket brings a sense of security when traveling. Mental constructions are not reality, however. There is danger in forgetting this. Cooperrider and Srivastva (1987) remind us of the capacity we have to be led astray by theories; how we can use them to uphold our prejudices, to deny contradictory evidence, to defend our hypotheses, and to deceive ourselves and others by giving comfort in thinking we "know the truth." They use the powerful example of the work of Morton, (as related in Gould, 1981), who was praised by the *ew ork Times* at the time of his death in 1851: "Probably no scientific man in America enjoyed a higher reputation among scholars throughout the world than Dr. Morton." This researcher hypothesized that by measuring the cranial volume of skulls of different races, mental and moral capacity could be determined, and he was out to prove it. He concluded, after much collecting and measuring, what he and those citizens with the highest status wanted to hear: that whites are superior. (Teutons and Anglo Saxons *most* superior.) Cooperrider and Srivasta write:

> The problem with these conclusions–as well as the numerical data which supported them–was that they were based not on "fact" but purely and simply on cultural fiction . . . Theory is not only a shaper of expectations and perceptions. nder the guise of "dispassionate inquiry" it can also be a peddler of values, typecasting arbitrary value as scientific "fact." (p. 145)

I think it obligatory that we give thought to how we are, or may be, affected by the culture of our profession. What are we not seeing when we look through the frames supplied to us by others? What do we lose by using the simplifications of individual diagnoses rather than considering the system and the larger field of the individual to help orient us in our work? What might we learn were we to keep a field perspective when considering the how and why of the creation of the DSM itself?

The point is not that there is something wrong with the American Psychiatric Association creating the DSM-IV. In the medical profession it is fitting to have a book that describes pathology. In the medical tradition, however, there are also a plethora of books describing treatment modalities for specific pathology. (At one time bloodletting and applying leeches were treatments commonly used.) But for MFTs, in the context of the less precise social science of marriage and family relations, it seems to me the danger is in draping a client in a diagnosis. This is contrary to a holistic approach that requires us to see, hear and consider the whole person, and also to take a look through a wide angle lens to view the system and the larger field of which the system is a part. True, the diagnosis may give us a convenient handle to grasp. Then the question must be asked: is this a way to better serve our client? Or is this simply a way of maintaining a concept of ourselves as capable practitioners by helping us feel more "scientific," comfortable and competent to speak about a case? We can settle on the diagnosis, we can fall back on unexamined hypotheses or theories, whether they be implicit or explicit; and we can know how to describe in psychiatric terms what is amiss. Do we then "know what to do?" As the saying goes, "For those who have a hammer, the problem always tends to be a nail."

Polanyi (1958) wrote: "the gain in exactitude, resulting from a stricter elimination of ambiguities, is accompanied by a loss of clarity and intelligibility" (p. 119). He was speaking of mathematics. (Polanyi adds the footnote, "We may recall here also that legal documents and government regulations, which are carefully worded to achieve the greatest precision, are notoriously unintelligible.") When we eliminate ambiguities in respect to human beings, which is a danger in using a diagnosis as a description of a person, we lose all humanness. Surely this influences the thinking, behaving, and interaction then generated in dealing with a client. And what of the therapist's humanness? Our humanness is the best handle we have; granted it is not the easiest.[1]

SCIENCE AND ART

Psychotherapy has two important components: science and art. The April, 1996, issue of the   *ational   esear her* carried an article I think speaks directly to the issue of art and science in such fields as education and psychotherapy. The article "The Relationship Between Theory and Practice: Back to the Classics," by Kessels and Korthagen, deals with the differences between abstract knowledge–knowledge as *episteme* (Plato's ideal)–and practical wisdom or concrete skills–knowledge as *phronesis* (Aristotle's view). Epistemic knowledge is cognitive; for example, it has to do with scientific understanding, theory, knowledge that is considered "proven" by research–usually thought to be "objective." It is basically conceptual knowledge. Because a theory, to be useful, must be applicable in many situations, it must be fairly general and abstract.

In contrast to scientific understanding is knowledge as *phronesis*, a different type of knowledge, (the Greeks recognized several types), that the authors describe as practical wisdom. It is essentially *per   ept al* instead of   *on ept al*. They quote from Aristotle: "It must take into account particular facts, since it is concerned with practical activities, which always deal with particular things" (Kessels   Korthagen, 1996, p. 19; Aristotle,   *i   th.*, Book VI, 1141a-b). This I think is the most important: Aristotle recognized that both kinds of knowledge are necessary, but it is the ability to perceive the particular facts in a particular situation that is critical; and even without abstract or theoretical knowledge people can excel in responding to problems in a concrete, present reality. So rather than turning to expert knowledge in the form of rules and/or theories, perceptual knowledge provides what is most essential: that is, information based on what is actual in a present situation. I maintain that much of what is taught as theory and practice is based on abstractions of rules and choices of behavior that have evolved from others' practical experiences. But their actual situations, although perhaps similar in some ways, cannot be identical to the situations in which we find ourselves. That which is most appropriate in a situation is our own response to what is real in our moment.

I want to stress that there is no suggestion that one or the other form of knowledge is sufficient. However, there is a tendency to lose ourselves in the episteme form, to imagine that problems can be handled if we can only apply the right theory. On this topic of rules and theories (episteme) the authors write: "This knowledge can also be used as an instrument for exploration of one's perceptions; it can generate questions, points of view, arguments and such. The pitfall, however, is to consider it as more than an instrument for exploration-as the thing itself that we are after, the real thing. For the real thing is not conceptual knowledge, episteme" (Kessels and Korthagen, 1996, p. 21). Finally, what makes perceptual knowledge–phronesis–of utmost importance is that, unlike theories and abstractions, practical knowledge is what taps into the humanness of each of us, for it includes "emotions, images, needs, values, volitions, personal hang-ups, temper, character traits and the like" (Kessels   Korthagen, 1996, p. 2).

Having an acquaintance with theories, though they be abstract and general, gives a basis that can help organize concepts and general rules, that can make practical knowledge more useful, that facilitates a more flexible movement between figure (the couple, their interaction, for example) and ground (what you know about them from previous meetings or moments of the present meeting, your experience as a therapist, for example)–an ability to recognize which details within a situation are more likely to have significance. The episteme, while having importance, is severely limited in practice, as I suppose many of us have found in our own experience. Theory provides ground for practice. It adds meaning to the experiences of practice, moment by moment. However, should theory become so important to the practitioner that it becomes figure and is substituted for actual experience, then it interrupts contact between therapist and client and thus interferes with process,[11] leaving little space for art, for using ourselves as our most important instrument. In my experience in training and supervision, I find my students and supervisees have little knowledge as phronesis. Their abilities to perceive and grasp what is needed from moment to moment, to use emotions to deepen and enrich their work, is sorely lacking.

AN INTERACTI N

As I write this, today's newspaper reports the victory of Deep Blue, the chess playing computer, beating the world champion human player, Gary Kasparov. "I lost my fighting spirit," were the defeated champion's words. The humanness of each of us is our strength and sometimes our downfall. In the practice of counseling or therapy it is the source that supplies what no theory or therapy machine could ever provide: the human interaction. What is the ingredient that makes us laugh harder when we read something aloud to share it with another? What is it that increases our sorrow when reading something sad to another that would not elicit tears when read silently? What is this contagion of emotions when people share themselves with one another? We experience it during rituals when experiences are shared and emotions are heightened. What happens when a couple in therapy speak directly from their experience in the moment to one another rather than to the ceiling, the floor or the therapist? There is "self disclosure" (Jourard, 1964). Their words are accompanied with feelings, with the expressions of emotion, perhaps barely perceptible; it is this quality that penetrates the fortress within which each had protected herself or himself. There comes a moment when personal agenda no longer fans the argument, a moment when emotional distance shrinks, the ephemeral, fleeting fraction of a second when they participate in a shared consciousness–unrehearsed, unplanned, unexpected. They see one another and recognize pain: there is contact. Perhaps shared tears, perhaps shared laughter. The practical experience of the therapist in perceiving and responding is the key to modeling and facilitating such interaction.

Reading Minuchin (1996) is a reminder that there are times we "do" by not doing and "help" by not helping; and like a homeopathic cure, paradoxical interaction may best be treated with paradox. About one supervisee, he comments: " She needed to incorporate uncertainty into her style–the capacity not to know, the capacity not to act." How does one learn to tolerate uncertainty? How does one teach the capacity not to act? Such skills come from practical experience, from our human sensibilities, from others' example. They most often stem from implicit knowledge that is never even verbalized. They seem to be connected to spontaneity, authentic responses to what is happening in the moment, when contact with oneself and the other happens simultaneously to create what Heshusius (1994) referred to as *parti i patory ons io sness*. Often we express our humanness in moments unfettered by conscious conceptualizing, or by trying, or by deliberation, at the times when we are, as expressed in the letter of de Vries (see above) "set free of knowing" what a client needs and how we must provide.

Those currently practicing marriage and family therapy have the advantages of building on the creativity and originality of pioneers such as Satir, Whitaker, Bowen, Minuchin, Haley and others. Their genius was in their "tacit knowledge," ways they connected and used themselves creatively to facilitate what Bateson called *se on or er hange*. Via their originality and courage they influenced family members to relate differently to one another. We have the good fortune to learn from and be inspired by these people and the many others who have been our teachers. In addition there are journals and conferences and e-mail lists, a rapidly growing body of information on the development of and the use of various therapeutic approaches. And beyond all this, to trust ourselves, use ourselves and discover our own art.

Dependence on a diagnosis of a pathological condition for payment has important consequences for both psychotherapist and the couples (and families) they treat. What might be the reactions, spoken or unspoken, that a client has on learning she or he has the status of a diagnosis? For some clients it may be taken as a kind of boon, of relief: "Well, there's a name for what's been wrong with me all these years. Imagine that. You see, dear, it's not my fault I get like this. I have this diagnosis. Now people will understand me better." For some clients learning they have an officially described dysfunction may seem to aggravate the problem: "Boy, this sounds serious. I didn't realize I have an actual illness. Does this mean I'm crazy? Doctor, can you do something for me? Or is there a pill I can take? And all the time I thought you (to the spouse) were the problem and I was fine." A diagnosis can be a serious disadvantage when the records, which are not confidential in the hands of an HMO, jeopardize a client's job. Or when an insufficient number of paid therapy visits are allowed for a given diagnosis.

T E   D NE S AND N T S   D

The current outlook of couple's therapy seems to be a mixed one. In recent years large segments of the population have learned through the media that going to a professional for help in resolving marriage problems is not disgraceful or an indication of severe mental disorder. In addition, mental health benefits specifically for marriage and family therapy have become available under some health insurance policies. These factors, in large measure due to the efforts of the national and state organizations of marriage and family practitioners, have been instrumental in helping the profession to grow. Yet the vision of full schedules and generous income has little to do with the reality of many MFTs, especially in areas of the country where there is a preponderance of therapists with this specialty. Articles in state and national journals have appeared presenting a picture of fewer clients for couples and family therapy.

In their newsletter, *Family Therapy ews* (Feb. 1997), The American Association for Marriage and Family Therapy published survey results of nearly 1, mental health providers which show that one-third of psychotherapists are finding it necessary to augment their income with second jobs. Sixty-two percent of psychotherapists reported a drop in income, and 55 of MFTs and social workers alike. Managed care rates are approximately 16 off "usual and customary rates." In terms of income of MFTs, only 22 comes from managed care, 55 from private pay clients, and the rest from other third-party insurers or contract work. "Fifty-four percent of the therapists surveyed said managed care has made mental health services more affordable and 52 said it has increased therapists' accountability" (*Family Therapy ews*, Feb. 1997). In these tougher times many therapists have evening and weekend hours.

> For the first time there seems to be a necessity for broadening the scope of practice; for finding ways to use our expertise outside of the usual practice as we have defined it. Negative influences affect all of us in ways we had not anticipated. In some areas there are simply not enough clients to go around. Some therapists are discouraged by having to deal with HMOs, the regulations, the paper work, and low fees. (*Family Therapy ewsletter*, Feb. 1997)

So much in today's therapy environment–especially the influence of HMOs–exemplify the tail wagging the dog phenomenon, where we are not our own agents but the pawns of others who, although they are not experts in our field, are making decisions that affect us. Do we know what kind of education and training we need to help our clients; indeed, do we know what actually helps our clients? In their introduction to a special issue of the *o rnal o Marital an Family Therapy*, Sprenkle and Bailey (1995) wrote, "If our discipline is to remain a viable 'player' in the health care system, it will be necessary to demonstrate our effectiveness both clinically and financially" (p. 339). There seems to be an increase in research attempting to accomplish this: to determine the efficacy of different approaches of therapy for family and couple interventions, taking into consideration the type of disorder or disfunction present. What has been demonstrated is the complexity of the various research studies reported and the difficulty of drawing categorical conclusions. However, Guest Editors Pinsof and Wynne (1995) stated:

> Marital and family therapists and researchers can justifiably feel heartened by the considerable accumulated evidence reviewed here on the efficacy of marital and family therapy for specific disorders in specific populations. Our field is healthy, strong, and growing. In almost every area reviewed, outcomes have been found as good as or better than other approaches to psychotherapy. (o rnal o Marital an Family Therapy, p. 342)

I think of early family therapists, the originals, whose work is still instrumental and influential in the field of marital and family therapy. They interacted with families, each in her or his own manner, according to their subjectivity,[1] their histories and personalities. They "mapped" families (Minuchin, 1996) and intervened on the basis of hypotheses that sprang from their own experience and the concrete situation at hand. They were dealing with people in the moment, in the now. Diagnoses and theories may be aids to the practitioner; however, I fear they may also put up barriers, limit creativity and especially contact, between therapist and clients. When all is said and done, after we study the s ien e the theories, approaches, and interventions of those who have come before us–we develop our self and our *art*. Having teachers who use participatory, interactive methods which include self-scrutiny and awareness can help lay the foundations.[1] It is through art that we express ourselves and allow our creativity to blossom. It is through who we are, expressed in our art, that we can best be of help to those couples who come to us.

Working with couples today may be considered more "scientific" than earlier, but as practitioners we must do justice to human complexities and paradoxes and let go of the idea of "exact" science. With care and openness we listen to people's stories, understand and acknowledge their pain, create potential bridges for them where they can meet one another if and when they are ready to take those steps. We provide tools and facilitate what couples need and have always wanted, from the time of folktales up to the present: to experience sharing life with an ally–not an enemy; to live in harmony, to feel loved and cherished; to *omm ni ate* in the best sense of the word, be intimate, and enjoy one another in the process of sharing life's experiences.

A THOR NOTE

Judith . rown has been in private practice in Santa arbara, CA for over twenty years. For close to thirty years she has been a trainer and supervisor, conducting workshops with her husband, eorge I. rown, in the U.S. and abroad. She is the author of books on marriage and family issues. Her most recent book is *The I in Science: Training to Utili e Su ectivity in Research*, published by Scandinavian University Press, 1996. A new edition of her first book, *Back to the Beanstalk: Enchantment and Reality for Couples*, is forthcoming in spring, 1998, by estalt Institute of Cleveland Press, 1 88 Ha el Drive, Cleveland, OH 106.

NOTES

1. Daly (1996) likens the experience of families trying to fit into a day what seems to require at least a week to H. . Wells description in *The Time Machine*: As I put on pace, night followed day like the flapping of a black wing. . . . I saw the sun hopping swiftly across the sky, leaping it every minute, and every minute marking a day. Daly adds, ike the time traveler, we seem to be putting on pace (p. 13).

2. This describes the middle-class situation. Among lower class families, more fundamental survival issues of sufficient food, decent housing, and health care often predominate.

3. According to the SE (oard of ehavioral Science Examiners), as of April 2, 1998. In California our official designation is Marriage, Family and Child Counselors.

. Most advances of 20th-cent. medicine are attributed to a paradigm know as the bio-medical model, which incorporates mind-body dualism and a reductionist approach with the aim of identifying a single external cause or cure for each specific disease (Pincus, 1996). A ationale for Studies of Spontaneous emission *Advances: Journal of Mind Body Health.* Vol.12, No. 1. Winter 1996. eview of *Spontaneous Remission: An Annotated Bi liography*, by rendan O egan and Caryle Hirshberg.

. I include couples therapy in the larger, more comprehensive category of family therapy.

6. uote from letter of Don Ephron, ondon, Ontario, in Memories of Harry oolishian, edited by Harlene Anderson, Ph.D. and ermaine Welch, Ph.D. *The amily Therapy News* is an organ of the AAMFT.

7. A look through the library data base of ournal articles listed under the sub ect words couples counseling showed the following, the first ten in order: (1) Holiday Therapy 101, Marriage Counseling for ay Couples (1996). (2) Thirty-five ear Old Pregnant Women Considering Maternal Serum Screening and Amniocentesis (1996). (3) A eview of Comprehensive uestionnaires used in Premarital Education and Counseling. ( ) Vail of Tears: The Church Is Part of our Divorce Problem–and Solution. ( ) We Can t Control Our Son. (6) The Infertile Couple. (7) Easing the oss: Predicting Miscarriages. (8) Suffer the Children. Woody Allen–Mia Farrow custody fight (1993). (9) Can I Trust My Husband A Husband Drinking Problem (1992). (10) Frantic. After AIDS news she becomes a crusader (1992). Other topics that followed were: infertile couples, career-couple challenge, sex and the modern black couple. Under the sub ect words couple therapy were the following: (1) Unsexing the Couple. Couples therapy: feminine perspective (1996). (2) esearch Assessing Couple and Family Therapy (199). (3) The Affective ond: The oal of Couple-Centered Therapy. ( ) A Horneyan Analytic Perspective on Couple Therapy: a case study (199). ( ) Structured Couple Therapy in the Treatment of Inhibited Sexual Drive. (6) Enhancing the Treatment and Prevention of Depression in Women: The role of integrative behavioral couple therapy. (7) The oles of Conflict Engagement, Escalation and The feminine perspective (1996). Avoidance in Marital Interaction: a longitudinal view of five types of couples. (8) ender and Conflict Structure in Marital Interaction: a replication and extension (1993). (9) America s Angriest Home Videos: behavioral contingencies observed in home reenactments of marital conflict (1993). (10) Power and Violence: the relation between communication patterns, power discrepancies, and domestic violence (1993).

8. The authors have noted potential limitations of the study and areas for further research.

9. This quotation is from an e-mail communication. My request to include it was met with this reply: I d like to be quoted as the source, along with e-mail address so people can contact me if they want to respond. bobby a starnet.com (obert Feldhaus).

10. De Vries brought the following to my attention: in the field of medicine, resources are expended for what doctors and researchers can know. For example, a great deal of money has been expended on developing drugs to lower cholesterol rather than changing life-style which has been proven more relevant to development and outcomes of cardiovascular disease. More attention is paid to the disease than to the host–the person. This we must avoid in marriage and family therapy studies and therapy.

11. y *process* I refer to moving through experience moment by moment with openness to and awareness of what emerges, and with no controlling direction to reach a desired end-point or outcome.

12. I see sub ectivity as neither positive nor negative. It is a mental construction, a term that encompasses *human factors*, that is all that pertains to an individual: thoughts, emotions, feelings: the mind and the senses, the head, heart, body and soul (rown 1996).

13. See rown (1996) for an example of confluent education, where the sub ectivity of the students is considered the ma or sub ect matter of the course described.

REFERENCES

Amsel, arry, M.D. (1997), Corporate healthcare. *Tikkun,* , (3) 19-26.

Anderson, H. Welch, . (eds.) (1992), Memories of Harry oolishian. *amily Therapy News, 3,* 19.

rown, J. . (1996), *The I in Science: Training to Utili e Su ectivity in Research.* Oslo: Scandinavian University Press.

rown, J. . (1997), esearcher as instrument: An exploration of the relationship between gestalt and qualitative methodology. *Gestalt Review* , (1) 71-8 .

Conley, M. A. Miles, . . (1997), Forging a new trail: Emerging trends for MFTs. *The California Therapist,* , (1) 8.

Cooperrider, D. . Srivasta, S. (1987), Appreciative inquiry in organi ational life. *Research in Organi ational Change and Development,* , 129-169. reenwich, CT: JAI Press.

Denton, W. H., Patterson, J.E. Van Meir, E. S. (1997), Use of DSM. in marriage and family therapy programs: Current practices and attitudes. *Journal of Marital and amily Therapy, 3,* 81-86.

Daly, . J. (1996), *amilies and Time: eeping Pace in a Hurried Culture.* Thousand Oaks, CA: Sage Publications.

ould, S. J. (1981), *The Mismeasure of Man.* New ork: Norton and Company.

Heshusius, . (199), Freeing ourselves from ob ectivity: Managing sub ectivity or turning toward a participatory mode of consciousness *Educational Researcher, 3,* (3) 1 -22.

Jourard, S. M. (196), *The Transparent Self.* New ork: D. Van Nostrand Co.

essels J. and orthagen F. (1996), The relationship between theory and practice: ack to the classics. *The Educational Researcher, 5* (3) 17-22.

eslie, . S. (1997), egislative report. *The California Therapist,* (2) 6-10.

Minuchin, S., ee, W- ., Simon, . M. (1996), *Mastering amily Therapy: Jour neys of Growth and Transformation.* New ork: John Wiley Sons, Inc.

Pincus, T. (1996), A ationale for studies of spontaeous remission. *Advances: Jour nal of Mind Body Health,* , (1) 6 -69. eview of *Spontaneous Remission: An Annotated Bi liography.* y rendan O egan and Caryle Hirshberg.

Pinsof, W. M. Wynne, . C. (199), The effectiveness and efficacy of marital and family therapy: Introduction to the special issue. *Journal of Marital and amily Therapy,* , 3 1-3 2.

Polanyi, M. (19 8), *Personal nowledge: Towards a Post Critical Philosophy.* Chicago: University of Chicago Press.

Sprenkle, D. H. ailey, C. E., (199), Editor s introduction. *Journal of Marital and amily Therapy,* , 339-3 0.

Wiener, C. . Wysmans, W. M. (1990), *Grounded Theory in Medical Research: rom Theory to Practice.* Amsterdam: Swets eitlinger.

Integrative Psychotherapy
in the Current Managed Care Environment:
Does It Work with Couples?

Richard Erskine
Janet Moursund

SUMMARY. ontact internal, with the self, and e ternal, with others
is growth-enhancing. hen couples improve their ability to be contactful with each other, both their relationship and their individual level of
emotional well-being are likely to improve. ntegrative Psychotherapists help couples to deepen their level of contact by teaching them to
utilize in uiry, attunement, and involvement in their transactions with
each other. The authors discuss teaching these skills to couples, in the
conte t of eight common relational needs that must be responded to if a
relationship is to survive and grow. An e tensive clinical e ample is
provided. *Article copies availa le for a fee from The Haworth Document
Delivery Service: 8   34   678. E mail address: getinfo haworthpressinc.
com   e site: http: www.haworthpressinc.com*

ichard Erskine, PhD, is Director of the Institute for Integrative Psychotherapy in
New ork City and conducts training programs in both the United States and interna-
tionally. He is the author of numerous articles on the theory and practice of psychotherapy and co-author (with Janet Moursund) of *Integrative Psychotherapy in Action*
(estalt Journal Press, Highland, N   1997. IS N 0-989266-32-6).

Janet Moursund, PhD, is Associate Professor in the Department of Applied   e-
havioral and Communication Sciences at the University of Oregon. She is the author
of a number of textbooks in the areas of educational psychology, psychotherapy,
personality theory, and statistics, and is co-author (with   ichard Erskine) of *Integra
tive Psychotherapy in Action* (estalt Journal Press, 1997).

[Haworth co-indexing entry note]: "Integrative Psychotherapy in the Current Managed Care nviron-
ment: oes It Wor with Couples " rs ine, ichard, and Janet Moursund. Co-published simultaneously in
Journal of Couples Therapy (The Haworth Press, Inc.) Vol. 8, No. 3/4, 1999, pp. 5 - 3; and: *Couples
Therapy in Managed Care: Facing the Crisis* (ed: Barbara Jo Brothers) The Haworth Press, Inc., 1999,
pp. 5 - 3. Single or multiple copies of this article are available for a fee from The Haworth ocument elivery
Service [1-8 -34 -9 8, 9: a.m. - 5: p.m. (ST). -mail address: getinfo haworthpressinc.com].

KEYWORDS. ontact, in uiry, attunement, involvement, relational needs

All too often, traditional psychotherapy and managed care have been seen as mutually exclusive. Here in the   S, at least, the two approaches live side-by-side in a state of grudging tolerance at best, or outright hostility at worst. Yet practitioners from both camps use many of the same methods and techniques. It seems logical that each might profit from listening to the ideas and sharing the successes of the other. This is especially true in the area of couple therapy, since even in traditional therapy couple work tends to be relatively short-term.

In Integrative Psychotherapy, we teach couples how to make their relationship contactful. We provide them with a way to understand themselves and each other, to be fully present with each other–in short, to build the kind of relationship which is in and of itself thera-peutic. The skills and structures for doing this can be taught within a time-limited framework, and the approach is thus quite suitable for managed care as well as for pay-for-service settings.

Integrative Psychotherapy, as we understand and practice it, utilizes a broad range of theoretical bases. Integrative Psychotherapy differs from a general eclecticism ("if it works, use it!") in that it incorpo-rates each idea, each technique, each treatment plan, within its own carefully developed frame of reference. At the core of that frame of reference is the notion that interpersonal contact, as experienced in relationship, is a central factor in psychological well-being. If there is a deficit in someone's psychological health, Integrative Psychotherapy assumes that damaged relationships are also present. Similarly, we assume that healing these damaged relationships, and providing stable and healthy new ones, helps clients to recover their psychological well-being. To the degree that contact-in-relationship is present, psy-chological health will be enhanced. And this principle holds for all relationships: for parents and children, for couples, for friends, for therapists and their clients–long- or short-term.

The notion of healing through relationship is particularly relevant for couple therapy, where the couple's relationship is accepted at the outset as the focus of treatment. While it is often the case that one or both members of a couple can benefit from individual psychotherapy, and the ideal treatment would include opportunities for individual work, a third "client" in couple therapy is the relationship itself. As couples learn how to be increasingly contactful, how to listen and respond to and nurture each other, the relationship changes; over time, these changes may significantly diminish the need for individual therapy.

elational ee s A primary factor in couple dysfunction is the failure to meet each other's relational needs. In order to understand how to remedy that failure, the couple–and the therapist!–need first to understand that relational needs are experienced by everyone; they are present every day of one's life. They are not "abnormal" or "pathological" or "immature." They are a part of being human. Our relational needs lie in the background of our experiencing; when one of them emerges into awareness, and is satisfied, it naturally returns to background again. When unsatisfied, however, it remains; over time, such an unsatisfied need can taint and warp nearly all aspects of a relationship.

We have noticed eight relational needs which tend to come up over and over again in our work with individuals and couples. There are probably others, but these eight are the most common: (1) *se rity*, the need to be physically and psychologically safe with the other person; (2) *al ing*, the need to have the function of our behaviors recognized and valued; (3) *a eptan e* by a strong, dependable, protective other; (4) *m t ality*, knowing that the other person has had the same or similar experiences; (5) *sel e inition*, support for one's efforts to express one's individuality and uniqueness; (6) *to ha e an impa t* on the other person; (7) *to ha e the other initiate*, rather than always having to make the first move oneself; and (8) *to e press lo e* for the other. You will notice that "to be loved" is not on this list of relational needs–it is unnecessary, because when all of the other relational needs are met, this is precisely the experience of being loved.

When one or more of the relational needs is consistently unmet, the whole relationship is affected. Like an itch that can't be scratched, the unmet need becomes more and more demanding. It transforms from annoyance to pain, from pain to fixation. The person experiencing this pain tries to solve the problem, using the sorts of strategies that have worked in other situations. When these strategies prove ineffective, the person is likely to resort to older and more child-like coping mechanisms: what the Gestalt theorists refer to as "fixed gestalten" and the transactional analysts recognize as "script behaviors." The person may regress, behavior is likely to become more archaic, and perception of the partner is increasingly a function of the person's own projections.

And what is the partner doing, while all this is going on? Why, experiencing that his/her own relational needs are not being met, trying to cope, going through the same process. It's an interactive downward spiral, with each partner reacting to the ineffective behaviors of the other. The pattern is a familiar one for all couple therapists. Our problem as therapists is to reverse the pattern, and to do so within the relatively short time often available when working with couples.

Fortunately, Integrative Psychotherapy provides an answer, a means of reversing that downward spiral so that the couple can begin to support each other rather than dragging each other down. It's not a panacea, not a "guaranteed cure"–but it is an approach that is understandable, workable, conceptually simple, and surprisingly effective.

T E INTE RATI E S C T ERA   DE

Our model of a troubled relationship suggests that such relationships have two primary characteristics: one or both partners tend, when trouble arises, to *pro e t* (that is, to define the other partner in terms of past relationships) and to *regress* (to use increasingly primitive problem-solving strategies). It stands to reason that anything that will replace these two responses with more satisfying and effective ones is likely to reverse the deterioration in the relationship. The replacement that we have found to be most useful is that of *in iry*.

The at re o n iry Inquiry, of course, is the stock-in-trade of the psychotherapist. As professionals, we are taught how to ask questions directly, and how to use body language and declarative statements to ask them indirectly. We are taught to phrase our interventions so that they fit most usefully within the client's frame of reference, and how to time them so that the client is most likely to respond in a way that will be helpful. And we have learned that inquiry, skillfully done, informs both therapist and client; it encourages self-exploration and strengthens the therapeutic relationship.

Let's think, for a moment, about how inquiry connects with the eight relational needs we listed earlier. Imagine that you are a client, in couple therapy with your partner. Your therapist is teaching you to inquire, helping both of you to make sure that the process respects and acknowledges each of the relational needs:

e   rity There must be a clear agreement between the partners that the inquiry process won't be used, now or later, as a weapon. If you can believe that your partner won't use your self-revelation against you, you can gradually begin to feel safer with that partner; as you feel more and more safe, you will reveal more and more–and, in doing so, learn more about yourself as well. Your partner, in turn, is likely to feel increasingly safe as you demonstrate your trust and your willingness to be vulnerable.

al ing To have someone inquire about your internal experience, show interest, and refrain from criticizing you or solving your problems for you, is to feel valued. We teach our clients to assume that everything his or her partner does or says has an important positive function, even though that function may not be self-evident, and to frame their inquiry so as to tease out that function. Thus inquiry is not inquisition, not interrogation, but a genuine attempt to understand and participate in the other's experience.

eptan e by a strong, protective, dependable other. It can be hard to be strong and protective and dependable when your partner is saying things that you don't want to hear–it's much easier to leap in and start the old familiar battle all over again! Part of inquiry is remembering that we are asking about what the other person experiences, not about what "really" happens. When your partner listens with interest and respect to something with which he or she disagrees, hearing your story as simply your account of what went on inside of you, that partner will be able to be protective and dependable–and you will experience him or her as such.

M t ality Skillful inquirers know how to strike a balance between expressing mutuality ("I've felt exactly the same thing!") and keeping the focus of the inquiry on their partner. They also know how to find a related experience–often from fantasy, or dreams–to create mutuality when they haven't actually been in the same situation. Your partner's words and body language, as you tell your story, let you know that–in one way or another–he or she has been there, does understand, has shared that experience or can at least imagine it.

el e inition Here is where inquiry strikes right to the bull's-eye: more than anything else, it encourages and promotes self-definition. "How did you feel?" "What was that like *or yo* ?" "What did *yo* want from me?" By putting his or her own needs, wants, perceptions and beliefs aside for the moment, your partner focuses on your individuality, your uniqueness, without judgment or competition.

To ha e an impa t Inquiry as a one-way street will fail. As you begin to reveal more and more of yourself, you need to feel a response from your partner. You need to know that he or she has been touched in some way. When your partner shows this, by words or actions or body language, the need to have an impact is met. Again, as with mutuality, we teach members of a couple to show that they have been impacted while continuing to keep the focus on their partner.

To ha e the other initiate Inquiry, in a very real sense, *is* initiation. It's asking the question, rather than waiting to be told or ignoring the other person entirely. It's other-focused, rather than self-focused. When your partner comes to you, asks you about what is important for you, your need for his or her initiation is met.

To e press lo e Your partner inquires about your internal experience. If loving feelings are a part of that experience, you have the opportunity to express them. As inquiry proceeds, and gradually becomes a part of your natural relationship style, loving feelings between you and your partner are likely to increase; inquiry both encourages these feelings and allows for their expression.

Tea hing artners to n ire It sounds so simple: teach couples to inquire of each other. Teach them to shift the focus, to put their own needs and beliefs on hold for the moment. Teach them to ask questions, rather than to assume answers. Teach them to frame the inquiry in terms of their partner's internal experience, rather than in terms of "right" or "wrong." Teach them to take turns with their inquiry, so each has the opportunity to be the focus of the other's positive attention.

Of course, even though it may be simple, it's not easy. Couples bring a lot of baggage into their therapy: their own childhood history of needs-not-met, their accumulated resentments toward their partner, their fears of being abandoned, or controlled, or of being found unacceptable in some deep, too-awful-to-contemplate way, their projections, and their archaic coping strategies. Patiently, sensitively, respectfully, the therapist models the use of inquiry to explore all of this. And the exploration serves two purposes: it helps both partners to deal with the problems, and it demonstrates the skills which the partners will need when the therapist is no longer available to them.

So, how do we teach couples to inquire of each other in a therapeutic way? In order to answer that question, we need first to take a closer look at inquiry, at how it works and what are its components. With those elements in mind, we'll then move to a clinical example of a therapist "coaching" a client as she practices inquiring with her partner.

lements o onta t Inquiry is one of three essential elements–the most visible, and probably the most teachable–in creating contact-in-relationship. The other two elements are *att nement* and *in ol ement*; in a sense, these two are mirror images of each other. Attunement is the inquirer's sensitivity to his or her partner's ongoing experience: the partner's rhythm, emotions, developmental level, cognitive style, relational needs. Attunement guides and frames the inquiry process; implied and direct questions are constructed so as to match the partner's current state. If the partner is experiencing strong affect, for instance, feeling "little," needing support and validation, both the content and the style of the inquiry must take these things into account. uestions or statements that are highly cognitive, that require a rational or problem-solving response, that appeal to adult judgment and values, or that suggest challenge or criticism, won't be helpful. If the partner is doing a lot of internal processing, and needs time to reflect and "go inside," the inquiring partner must attune to that slower rhythm and slow down the pace of the inquiry. Attunement, then, involves literally being *in t ne* with the partner's experience, sensing what that experience requires, and providing what is needed.

"Sensing what that experience requires" brings us to *in ol ement*. If attunement is a kind of outward sensitivity, a focus on the partner, then involvement is the inward reciprocal: the willingness to respond internally to the partner, to be touched, to be vulnerable, to use all of one's knowledge and history and feelings to enhance one's understanding of the partner's experience. Involvement guides the inquiry, just as does attunement; indeed, they are intertwined and inseparable, for each informs the other. In so doing, they create *presen e*, the kind of being-with that is supportive, respectful, and contact-making.

We said earlier that inquiry is probably the most teachable of the three elements of contact-in-relationship. People can be taught how to frame direct questions, how to use voice tone or body language or a paraphrase to suggest a line of exploration. But attunement, too, can be taught: we can help couples to notice their partner's rhythmic patterns, to be aware of the moment-to-moment emergence of relational needs, to be sensitive to the level of affect or the degree of psychological regression that the partner is experiencing. Involvement is perhaps the most difficult to teach. It tends to emerge spontaneously as each partner begins to experience his or her own needs being met, and begins to feel safe enough to risk full contact with his or her own process. This leads to a kind of chicken-egg problem: if each partner needs to experience being inquired of therapeutically in order to be able to act as the inquirer, where does one start?

Fortunately, there is a third person involved here. The therapist inquires of each partner, modeling the process. When the partners are invited to inquire of each other, the therapist monitors them, and suggests appropriate moments to switch roles. We move in and out of the inquiry process, picking up the thread when the inquiring partner gets lost or confused or temporarily overwhelmed by his or her own emerging needs, and encouraging and/or prescribing the partners to take turns as inquirer and inquiree. A skillful couple therapist makes sure that *ea h* partner leaves the therapy hour with something for himself or herself, with a sense of having been heard, understood, and valued. And the benefit is threefold: each individual experiences contact (with the therapist and with the partner), is given a model for how to be therapeutic with the partner, and has an opportunity to practice the skills of inquiry.

As you teach couples how to inquire of each other, you will need to bring them back, over and over, to the basic focus of the inquiry: the partner's internal experience. Most couples find it very hard, at first, to maintain this focus. The inquiring partner may stray into establishing "reality" ("But it didn't happen that way!") or into self-defense ("I never said that!"), or may switch from a focus on the partner to an expression of his or her own views about the issue. The inquiree may become anxious, may misunderstand the questions, will often shift from internal experience to external events. And each of these sidetracks is a potential topic of inquiry in itself: "What happened for you just then?" "What was it like for you to have me say that?" "What are you wanting from me right now?"

For the therapist, assisting a couple in the inquiry process is a lot like juggling. There are so many balls to keep in the air–being attuned to each partner's emerging experience, staying in touch with one's own feelings and imaginings and sensations, tracking the pattern that's being created between the partners, attending to the technical details of effective inquiry, making decisions about if and when to encourage the partners to switch roles, or to move into the inquirer role oneself. But, as complicated and often confusing as it all may be, one thing is sure: you'll never lack for something to do in the session!

C INICA E A   E

For the last part of this paper, we would like to give you an example of inquiry as it is used in Integrative couple therapy. The segment below is transcribed from a tape recording of a five-day group composed of seven couples. It occurs during the third day, after all the participants have gotten at least an initial understanding of the nature of inquiry and how it can enhance a relationship. Betty and Sally, a lesbian couple, have asked for an opportunity to practice inquiry with each other, under Richard's supervision. Our comments are indicated in italics:

> *i har   the therapist   egins the segment with a   is   ssion o the   on ept o   presen e   an   its importan e in the in   iry pro ess This   is   ssion is partly   or the   ene it o all the parti i pants an partly to set the stage or the work that   etty an   ally are a o t to o*

Richard: Presence is really two-fold. And almost contradictory. I talk about "presence" as de-centering yourself. It's a way of making your own needs, your own desires, your own outcomes, your own knowledge, unimportant for a period of time. At the same time, however, to be present requires all the richness of our history, everything we've ever learned, everything we've ever read, all of our experiences, our own pains and agonies as well as our joys and pleasures. And it's a combination of going back and forth between the two, tapping into all of our experiences as a rich resource library, and then almost forgetting it and being totally present. And then coming back to it and using it as a resource to connect with the other. So it's that combination of free-associating within ourselves, to everything we've ever experienced, and then dropping it and focusing on the other.

I particularly wanted to emphasize that, Betty, because I think you have a history of forgetting yourself. Part of presence is knowing yourself fully, but then, for the moment, dropping it, as you center on the other. So with you I'm also going to emphasize the richness of your own history, that you bring to this relationship. Keep in mind, now, that if you're going to really inquire about her phenomenological experience, it's not about the content. It's about how she experiences it, the meaning she makes, what she feels, what she remembers . . . all the stuff that goes on inside her head, that we cannot observe. That we can only get by inquiring. (To Sally) Are you ready? For her to know you?

Sally: Yeah.

Richard: And for you to know you, through her knowing you?

Sally: Yeah, okay.

Betty: (pause, then softly) Where would you like me to begin knowing you? What part of you–

Richard: (interrupting) One question at a time! Your first question was just fine.

> *eginning in   irers o ten string se eral   estions together in an e ort to get it   st right or as a way o talking to themsel es a o t what they want to say Too many   estions at on e on t meet the relational nee   or se rity They   an   on se an   erail the partner who may get a ght p in trying to keep tra k o all the   estions an then   oesn t know whi h one to answer irst*

Sally: h, where would I like for you to start knowing me . . . (pause) I'm wondering if I'm confusing "where" with "when"?

Betty: Hmmm. (to Richard) I think that's why I started to rephrase the question.

Richard: Okay.

> *ow that   etty has   hara teri e her o le   estion as   re phrasing   i har   oesn t o e t   ally s omment s ggests that   etty may in ee nee to ome p with a   etter way to help ally egin to e plore her inner e perien e*

Betty: (pause, still very softly) Let me try another question. What part of you do you want me to get to know first?

Richard: (pause; Sally stares at her hands) Sally, what's really important here is your discovering your answer. It's not about a "right" answer. It's about your discovering of yourself, with her stimuli. (to Betty) Ask her the question again.

ensing that ally s ogniti e pro essing is getting in the way o reporting on her e perien e i har oa hes her on how to e an in iree is omment not only gi es her in ormation a o t what is e pe te o her t also gi es her permission to let go o her nee to e right an to look goo en a wrong answer is al e

Betty: What part of you do you want me to get to know first? Right now?

Sally: (pause) I just go blank.

Betty: Can you tell me what was in your hand when you were looking at it just now?

Sally: (somewhat sharply) I think it's the young part of me. Cause you only see the grown-up.

ally s tone o oi e len s an a satory ality to her statement an etty rea ts non er ally as i she has een riti i e To orestall a e ensi e response i har s ggests a new line o estioning

Richard: (to Betty) Now focus on what you do in your behavior, that she only gives you the grown-up. (pause) Just start, "What's my behavior that I only get the grown-up part of you?"

Betty: (carefully) What do I do that makes you only want to give me the grown-up part of you?

Sally: Whatever it was you just did then . . . Tone of voice, I'm not really sure, feels a bit patronizing. Feels a bit not sure what's going to happen next. Not sure whether you're going to be attacking, or turning . . .

Betty: Sort of like, what comes over in my voice isn't clear?

hile etty hasn t ite apt re ally s e a t meaning she is o sing on trying to apt re it rather than on e en ing hersel he is learning how to in ire

Sally: Intonation.

Betty: How does my intonation–

*etty ontin es along this line tho gh she may swit h the
o s rom ally s e perien e to her own To keep this rom hap
pening an   etty rom eeling riti i e   i har shares his
per eption an   makes a s ggestion*

Richard: (interrupting) Can I help you?

Betty: Yes.

Richard: I think what she's saying is the way you're cautious with her.
I think if you'd just talk much more matter-of-factly, and directly
. . . I know you're trying to be empathetic, right?

Betty: Yeah.

Richard: And you're trying to be protective.

Betty: Yeah.

Richard: I think when you get protective, she thinks something must
be wrong that you're being protective. And so she gets more
scared. Try just a matter-of-fact way of talking to her.

Betty: (laughing) Yeah . . .

Richard: Have you noticed that when I talk to her matter-of-factly, she
relaxes more? I think sometimes people who are used to protec-
tors trying to protect them from some terrible danger, um, respond to somebody's protective voice as though a danger must
exist. See what happens if you talk to her matter-of-factly.

Sally: (to Richard) Boy, that feels so much better! It's like, I was
waiting for the axe to fall . . .

Betty: (pause) (to Richard) Yeah, I don't very often . . . but I think I
forgot the question (chuckles).

Richard: "So what is it in my behavior that you don't like?"

Betty: (in a more conversational tone) What is it that I do, the way I
say things–

Sally: (interrupting) Well, you talk in intellectuals all the time. And it's
like you're creeping around. And then I think "what the heck is
she creeping around for? Does she think I'm going to explode, or
something else is going to happen? Do need to creep around?"
And I don't want to creep around. m . . . and it's like, like I
don't know whether you're going to shoot me or become a tiny
baby. Or that 2-year-old that stiffens her legs and goes "I-want-I-
want-I-want-all-of-you-I-want-all-of-you!" And you can't have
all of me. I don't *want* to give all of me to you.

*The matter o a t tone worke   ally is m h more animate
an more orth oming than she has een earlier lmost too*

m h so or   etty who now looks tear l   i har in ites her to
ret rn to in   iring rather than rea ting emotionally

Richard: (pause, then prompts Betty) "What o you want to give me?"

Betty: What . . .

Richard: Matter-of-fact!

Betty: Yeah. Okay. So what do you want to give me, then?

Sally: I want to give you *what* I want to give you *when* I want to give you!

Betty: And that–what is that?

Sally: I want to give you my excitement, and my creativity, and my craziness, and my sadness, and my anger; and I want, I want to give you . . . whatever I want to. But there has to be that bit that sometimes I don't want to give you all of me. I want to give to other people too.

etty s relational nee iness is growing to the point at whi h she may not e a le to maintain her o s on ally he may also imagine that she is eing riti i e an atta ke   while ally has e ome more om orta le an spontaneo s t s time or a swit h time or etty to e gi en a han e to e plore an e press her own e perien e

Richard: (to Sally) Now, you make an inquiry . . .

Sally: h . . . So how is that for you?

Betty: I'm really struggling to stay adult and stay in there.

Sally: Right . . .

Richard: (prompting Sally) "Tell me more about it . . . " This is decentering from *yo* now.

Sally: Yeah, yeah.

Richard: And making her the center.

Sally: m, so . . . Tell me more about that.

ally s willingness to ontin e o sing on etty rather than engaging in the s al str ggle a o t whose e perien e is the more ali or important en o rages etty to mo e more lly into her a e t

Betty: (close to tears) When you get big, and you start doing all those things . . . (pause) I think I become unimportant then. And I want to be important to you.

Sally: (whispers) And you *are* . . .

*ow i i   lt to stay with the partner s pro ess rather than   mp
ing in to ease their pain   ally s response to   etty s tear l long
ing is almost re le i e   t pain easing here is like the aspirin
that masks the symptoms o a   isease it an get in the way o
is o ering what is really happening   etty s primary relational
nee here is that o sel   e inition an   i har in ites ally to
atten to it*

Richard: (to Sally) Too much reality, too soon. Go three or four more inquiries about being important.

Sally: Okay. (to Betty) So, what does being important . . . So tell me about what being important means.

Betty: (sigh) It's taking time with me. And sharing an interest in what I do. Showing that I can do things, so that you can see that I can do things. And then it's getting all mixed up, because I'm getting all mixed up now between you and my mother. I know it. That's why I want you to do it, because she didn't do it.

Sally: So tell me what it is that I'm doing, to make you get mixed up.

Betty: (pause) I really like that question. I wish to God I could find the answer.

Sally: Just keep looking at me. My body? My voice? My eyes? My hands? Check me out.

Betty: It could be your voice . . . it could be your voice. It's not your hands, it's not things like that.

Sally: Okay.

Betty: You do what she does to me. You say, "Right, Betty, pull yourself together, and give me the right answer. Stop being a child and give me the right answer, cause you know what it is really." You do that to me. That's what I hear you doing to me. That's when I say "You're criticizing me."

*ally has een oing ery well   t here she in s hersel st k
he looks at i har with a what o o now e pression an
he helps her to mo e etty rom o o it into   nee some
thing*

Richard: (prompting Sally) "So are you saying what you need from me is . . . "

Sally: Ah. So you're saying you need for me not to say to you "Pull yourself together"?

Betty: I need for you not to expect me to get it right. Cause I don't always do it your way.

Sally: No, you don't.
Betty: That doesn't mean to say I'm wrong.
Sally: No, no. There is a "your way" and there is a "my way."
Betty: Yeah.

t k again   ally may e sli ing into sear hing or a sol tion to the pro lem or she may   e str ggling with her   esire to talk a o t her own e perien e or   e en her eha ior   hate er is going on or her it s taking her attention an her o   s away rom etty   en i har s prompt oesn t really ring her a k

Richard: (prompting Sally) "So are you saying . . . "
Sally: Yeah–God, this is hard! So are you saying . . . h . . . I don't know what to say here.
Richard: What is she saying to you? You've got to stay focused on her. What is she saying to you?
Sally: h . . . I'm going to get this wrong, wait a second . . . So are you saying to me that–

s the in irer st as when she was the in iree ally is on erne with getting it right he is rel tant to ent re a g ess that might not e orre t n her str ggle to in that right answer is inter ering with her o s on etty i har gi es the nee e permission

Richard: (interrupting) It's all right to get it wrong. Cause she'll correct you.
Sally: Yeah, I get it.
Richard: The question built into it is "Am I wrong?" So: "Are you saying . . . " and let her correct you. Assume you're wrong, and say it.
Sally: I don't know what the question is, though. I haven't got a question.
Richard: "Are-you-saying-"what did she say to you?
Sally: That sometimes she's going to get it wrong, and there's a "her way"–and no, she's not going to get it wrong. Her way isn't wrong.
Richard: "So are you saying that you want me to value your way? Even when it's different from mine?"
Sally: And it's really interesting, cause right now there's a little fight going on in me, Richard, saying "But I o do that."

This response is irt ally ine ita le i it isn t ma e o t lo it s e perien e internally y most partners somewhere in the in i

*ry pro ess   hen o r partners es ri e an e perien e that is
ontrary to o r own we almost a tomati ally mo e to arg e with
or orre t them This response tho gh is pro a ly more   estr
ti e o the in   iry pro ess than any other so i har mo es
igoro sly to rge ally to e enter an re o s on etty*

Richard: Drop it! Get out of your own experience. Get into hers.
(pause, then softly) Get out of your own experience. This is not
about reality; this is about her experience. Here is what doesn't
make the relationship work. Get out of your experience, Sally.
Right now make Sally not count.

Sally: But I've spent so long saying I *o* count!

Richard: I know. That's the first half of psychotherapy. This is the
second half. Go ahead, and keep it a question.

Sally: So, what you're saying is, what you're asking me to do, is to
value your way.

Richard: "Is that right?"

Sally: Is that right, or is that wrong?

Betty: Yes. I want you to do that.

Sally: Right. So, what would I be doing or saying so that you knew
that I was doing that?

Richard: Beautiful question!

*t was a ea ti l   estion Moreo er ally has han le   i h
ar s on rontation ery well in ee an his appre iation here is
also an a knowle gment o her willingness to p t hersel to one
si e an o s on etty*

Sally: (to Richard) See, I can do it!

Richard: I know you can! You've just got to make yourself not important for the time being.

This piece of work continues for quite a bit longer. There is no easy
stopping place for us: as in most good therapy, each statement flows
into the next and the entire piece of work becomes an organic whole.
So we've made an arbitrary and abrupt stop at this point, simply
because we are running out of space.

As indicated in the annotations, the transcript illustrates many of the
specifics of teaching couples how to inquire; it also illustrates a number of ways in which couples can get stuck, and how to "un-stick"
them. But, far more important than these technicalities, the transcript

gives an overall picture of the inquiry process with couples. Putting yourself in the place of either of the partners, imagining what that person's experience might be, will give you a sense both of the general flow of the process and the way in which relational needs emerge and can be met through careful, caring inquiry. And that is the essence of inquiry's healing and relationship-building potential: it allows each partner to meet the other's relational needs, to feel understood and valued and safe.

Inquiry needn't be–and usually isn't–the only intervention used in Integrative couple therapy, but it is one which fits nicely with many other approaches and within a variety of theoretical frameworks. It is particularly appropriate for the short-term work which managed care so often requires, in that its basics can be taught rather quickly, practicing it in the therapy session usually helps the couple begin to deal with their important relational issues (as we saw with Betty and Sally), and the couple leaves therapy with a tool that they can use on their own in the months and years to come.

How Managed Care
Can Help Couples Cope

James M. Shulman

SUMMARY. This article traces how managed care became a uick fi to curb out-of-control healthcare costs rather than a real effective approach to managing care. To date, the impact has been not only a negative e perience, but impediment to treating couples facing relationship and related problems. The author is optimistic about how managed care will evolve to recognize the importance of couples and family treatment as we enter the future with integrated systems of healthcare. The future will also re uire significant shifts in the thinking and practice patterns of providers and an emphasis on uality and outcomes. *[Article copies availa le for a fee from The Haworth Document Delivery Service: 8 34 678. E mail address: getinfo haworthpressinc.com e site: http: www.haworthpressinc.com*

KEYWORDS. Managed care, behavioural health care, eimbursements, integrated delivery systems

INTR D CTI N

When I was asked to address how managed care can help couples cope, my first thought was this will only take a paragraph. Managed

---

James M. Shulman, PhD, is Vice President, ehavioral Health of Mount Carmel Health System and Chief Executive Officer of Mount Carmel ehavioral Healthcare Company, a multi-disciplinary outpatient behavioral healthcare practice with over 0 full-time clinicians.

[Haworth co-indexing entry note]: "How Managed Care Can Help Couples Cope." Shulman, James M. Co-published simultaneously in *Journal of Couples Therapy* (The Haworth Press, Inc.) Vol. 8, No. 3/4, 1999, pp. 5-8 ; and: *Couples Therapy in Managed Care: Facing the Crisis* (ed: Barbara Jo Brothers) The Haworth Press, Inc., 1999, pp. 5-8 . Single or multiple copies of this article are available for a fee from The Haworth ocument elivery Service [1-8 -34 -9 8, 9: a.m. - 5: p.m. (ST). -mail address: getinfo haworthpressinc.com].

care, as it has been practiced in the last ten years, has tried to avoid providing services to couples. I am optimistic that this will change and that new opportunities will evolve for therapists who have expertise in couples and family treatment. This article reviews: (1) the reasons that managed care approaches have dominated behavioral healthcare service delivery in recent years; (2) why or how managed care has short-changed couples, and; (3) the new opportunities that will develop to serve couples.

T E REAS NS ANA ED CARE A R AC ES A E D INATED E A I RA EA T CARE SER ICE DE I ER

From the 196 s until the mid-198 s, psychiatrists, psychologists, social workers, marriage and family counselors, and other professionals grew in number and public acceptance. During this time most States enacted laws in licensing most of these professions and many also passed laws mandating insurance coverage for mental health vendors (Winegar, 1992). Where vendorship was not mandated, most States allowed psychiatrists and/or psychologists to supervise other professionals for insurance reimbursement. As independent practitioners proliferated, so did mental health services and the volume of insurance claims and third-party payments. Following legal mandates, insurance payors began covering outpatient mental health counseling services as well as inpatient treatment. ntil the mid-198 s these payors barely scrutinized services provided or claims paid. Consequently, without any review by payors, practitioners and treatment agencies experienced an "Age of Freedom" in healthcare reimbursement (Shulman, 1993). For practitioners treating couples, insurers reimbursed a number of diagnoses described in the American Psychiatric Association's *iagnosti an tatisti al Man al ol me* (DSM-II), with Transient Situational Disturbances (TSD)/Adjustment Disorders used most frequently. With the introduction of a revised diagnostic manual, e.g., DSM-III, those diagnoses which were used for reimbursement of couples treatment were no longer considered "true mental health" categories and were made into "V" codes which insurers began to exclude from reimbursement. Many practitioners quickly learned to bill under other less appropriate mental health diagnoses as the only way to receive insurance coverage for treating couples. At the same time that outpatient providers learned the new rules of reimbursement, inpatient providers also learned a number of "tricks of the trade." By the mid-198 s, the country saw an explosion of hospital programs for alcohol/drug treatment and psychiatric care which were designed around 3 -day stays, the magic number that most insurers would cover.

nfortunately, during this "Age of Freedom" abuses such as fraudulent billings and unnecessary treatment services became too frequent *Mo ern ealth are*, 8/4/97). For example, in the mid-198 s with uncontested insurance reimbursement, there was a rapid proliferation in the number of inpatient adolescent psychiatry units throughout the .S. that marketed programs to parents and encouraged them to admit an unruly adolescent for a short reprieve and the expense of the parents' insurer. Between 1982 and 1986 the number of adolescents in the .S. declined, but the incidence rates for their hospitalization went up 35 (Winegar, 1992). While inpatient providers were more obvious targets for abuse investigations, outpatient providers also came under greater scrutiny by payors for purported overutilization, potential abuse and weak or poor standards of practice (Feldman, 1992 and Austad, 1996).

In 1988 and 1989 the author's private practice was contracted by a number of major insurers to review outpatient claims and services of mental health/alcohol/drug providers. In reviews some of the questionable practices that we found included:

- Over a third of the providers who requested reimbursement did not have clinical or chart records with such basic information as a diagnosis, treatment plan, or progress notes for each session which are basic standards for good practice;
- Some non-medical clinicians had patients returning to see them weekly for as long as five years with no indication of any improvement in functioning. Reviewing psychiatrists found that many of these patients were diagnosed as depressed and had never been considered for or evaluated for antidepressant medication;
- Clinicians often used unsubstantiated diagnoses to meet insurance requirements and would change diagnoses if the original ones were not reimbursed;

- Many psychiatrists and psychologists were "selling their signature" to unlicensed, some non-degreed, practitioners by signing insurance forms as a supervisor for the patients when they (the supervisors) knew nothing about the patients;
- Many clinicians would waive co-payments and then fraudulently bill insurers for larger fees to cover patient services.

These type of activities along with the abuses by inpatient practices all contributed to the growth in healthcare costs affecting employers and insurers which lead to this country's recognition of a healthcare crisis in the late 198 s. The crisis set the stage for employers and insurers to create "managed care."

T E REI N   TERR R

The "Age of Freedom" for providers came to an end in the late 198 s. The healthcare (payer) industry shifted to the new paradigm of *manage   are.* Traditional health insurance or indemnity plans soon created new delivery systems that included Health Maintenance Organizations (HMOs), Preferred Provider Organization (PPOs), Independent Practice Associations (IPAs), Point of Service Plans (POS), and may other "alphabet models" of managed care. The original purpose of managed care was to develop a coordinated approach to the design, financing and delivery of health care. The goals were set to balance price and utilization controls with access to high quality care. Managed care plan designs specifically included such elements as limited access to providers, employment of utilization controls, higher levels of benefits available for "in-network" services, quality of care controls and the mutual establishment cost/utilization targets with employers and providers. Despite the original intent of managed care plans, much of the initial efforts by insurers and their agents really focused on managing costs and rationing care rather than on managing care.

By 199 the "Age of Freedom" for providers or providers shifted to the "Reign of Terror" (Shulman, 1993) where providers felt terrorized by payers, and what was called managed care was more often described as mismanaged or "mangled" care. Payers and their agents cut fees, held providers hostage to contract language, e.g., with gag rules, denied care, outright refusal or delayed payments and threatened providers who would not follow rules. This was particularly evident in the mental health and chemical dependency (MH/CD) treatment arena when payers "carved out" MH/CD treatment and bankrolled a whole new industry, i.e., managed behavioral healthcare. Early players applied the same techniques of utilization review and managed care plans as were being used in medical care and soon dominated the market of MH and CD treatment inventing a new label, i.e., behavioral healthcare. Providers no longer had the freedom to treat individuals, couples or families, without a "big brother" looming overhead, indicating what would or would not be covered. More was not covered rather than covered in most cases. Managed behavioral healthcare organizations initially selected the most inexpensive providers and facilities which demonstrated the briefest treatments independent of outcomes. Treatment was meted out on the basis of session-by-session or minimal numbers of sessions or inpatient days followed by "micro-management," i.e., cumbersome paper and adversarial telephonic reviews. Because the initial plans for HMOs, PPOs, or other types of self-insured plans, used the industry standards for covered service and exclusions used by traditional indemnity insurance plans, the benefits offered were as limiting as they were with non-managed care insurance companies. One improvement was that exceptions began to be made for intermediate care levels of treatment (day treatment, intensive outpatient groups, structured group programs, etc.) which insurers previously did not reimburse. Trade-offs of inpatient days for two or three day treatment days began to be written into new plans. However, in the treatment of couples, there was even less emphasis placed on looking at the whole family or couple, than had been under the old DSM TSD diagnoses. Managed care plans were much more skeptical about the reasons for couples approaching treatment and became even more rigid using the insurance standards that said couples' treatment was not a covered benefit. As noted earlier, many clinicians became shrewd and savvy and learned to define couples' treatment under the classification of an identified patient and would use a legitimate or reimbursable diagnosis. Individuals were able to obtain some couples' treatment with half of the couple being part of collateral visits. Where this was not easily accomplished, couples would become more frustrated with their insurance plans and the managed behavioral health care firms as authorizations and reimbursement for couples services would be denied. This became true for may other similar problems, e.g., requiring a family or parent-child treatment. The frequent denials for coverage put additional stress on couples and families. Many providers resenting managed care intrusion inappropriately egged patients on by encouraging vigorous protest to employers and payers and by "badmouthing payers." nfortunately, managed behavioral health care plans had some legitimacy in distrusting providers as many remained unfocused on their treatment, continued unnecessary utilization, kept poor or no (legally required) records and acted as if insurance coverage was a entitlement. The end result of managed care has left some individuals with untreated problems which in fact could lead to more serious emotional disorders, domestic violence, abuse, medical conditions, etc. Inciting patients also added stress to those who were able to get some authorizations for treatment. Many providers did learn to turn "lemons into lemonade" by either adopting more focused forms of treatment and/or developing non-insurance reimbursable programs to help individuals with couple, stress, work and other problems. Providers also developed Employee Assistance Programs (EAPs) which offer alternatives to insurance and strict interpretations of benefits. With many EAPs couples could have help in coping and not have to battle with managed care firms. In sum, managed care (itself) has not directly assisted most couples in their coping. However, unintentionally it has helped couples by setting the stage for some providers to become more focused in treatment. Many other providers who just couldn't work with managed care entities have also become entrepreneurial and developed alternatives such as EAPs, weekend couples' retreats, special educational programs, and a variety of other approaches with sliding fee schedules designed to help couples who can't afford costly 1:1 sessions.

CR STA   A   IN   T E   T RE
IS T ERE   I   E A   TER   ANA ED CARE

The future holds a number of "good news, bad news" scenarios for providers as well as patients, especially couples. The first bad news is that due to the increased competitiveness of managed care entities in the private sector things will be worse before they'll get better. Major players continue to fight for market share. The surplus of providers in the market place makes it even easier for managed care firms to continue to lower reimbursements. Some providers are actually being forced out of business, unable to earn a living. By the year 2   Nicholas Cummings, Ph.D., grimly predicts that 5   of current psychotherapists will be out of business (Cummings et al., 1996). Competition has resulted in many firms continuing forms of terrorism. However, the first good news for providers in the private sector is that for these firms to remain competitive and profitable, there is very little room left for them to grow and the payers are also squeezing them financially. As a result of decreasing profits, losses and lack of growth opportunity, the largest managed care companies have turned toward the public sector for future growth and development. In the public sector state governments are developing carveouts which are designed for managed behavioral healthcare companies to operate the statewide Medicaid programs. n-like in the private sector where huge profits and denial of services was largely unchecked by payers, the public programs do have limits on profitability and specific service targets. There is opportunity for profitability, but with greater built-in controls. For couples and families who are covered by Medicaid, the good news is that there may be greater opportunities for assistance and service than in a non-managed system. The bad news is for the private provider who treats or would like to treat Medicaid recipients. Without some connection with a publicly funded agency, e.g., community mental health center or hospital entity, there may be fewer opportunities. In most states with Medicaid managed care, the managed care organizations have partnered with or contracted with the large community agencies for services. The more these agencies are doing in the managed care arena the tougher the competition will be for providers in general. Throughout the country, publicly funded agencies with managed care know how are vying for private sector business. Many agencies are attractive to payers as they offer a larger array of services than independent providers. For providers who don't align themselves or contract with public funded agencies, there are still some, but limited, opportunities for longer term survival as noted earlier. For the patients such as couples seeking help, there may even be more opportunities. That's good news, but the bad news for independent providers is that they'll lose much of their autonomy, work for others and will have to work much smarter!

INTE RATED DE I ER S STE S

Throughout the country, managed care has set the stage for medical care providers to develop less expensive, higher quality and more integrated delivery systems. Ventures or partnerships between hospitals and physicians and sometimes even with payers, are resulting in reimbursements and incentives being better aligned. More effective application of new technologies, the use of advanced computer systems and the provision of more responsive, accessible care, suggest that these new ventures are preparing for the future. Many of the healthcare systems have true partnerships between individual providers and hospitals and in others the healthcare systems have developed or acquired specialty care providers including mental health and alcohol/drug agencies and individual providers. These for profit and not-for-profit integrated health delivery systems are cautiously developing their own capabilities to enter the market place as competitors to the managed care entities that grew from insurance firms in the 198 s and 199 s. In a number of urban markets employers have developed purchasing alliances which bypass insurance owned systems and directly contract with these emerging provider systems. These systems can reduce administrative costs and profit margins and also offer more divers and integrated services at lower costs than payers. Some systems have chosen to work tighter with the payers and avoid potential business loss through perceived or real competition with the payers. These provider systems negotiate preferred or exclusive arrangements with payers and seek partnerships that both focus on quality and align incentives through risk sharing models rather than accepting lower and lower fee-for-service amounts. In the behavioral health arena systems negotiate case rates to provide all services for certain diagnostic groups or agree to subcapitation rates for behavioral health services. Driven by the accreditation standards of the National Committee for uality Assurance (NC A), payers are seeking the providers who can best meet the standards, demonstrate quality or performance improvement, can service the whole patient and at the same time can provide required data and reports to support these efforts. In the future those provider based health systems that can also meet specific NC A behavioral healthcare standards, are prime for delegation of care by payers and managed behavioral healthcare entities required to meet such standards. This is welcomed good news, i.e., more local provider control in clinical delivery will someday return. The not so good (but not so bad) news is that the independent or private providers will have to become a part of these systems. For participation providers will need to stop wasting energy by "whining about the evils of managed care" and must direct it to practicing focused or targeted treatment, perfecting niche practice areas that minimize costly care, developing the ability to track positive outcomes and demonstrate client satisfaction, and quality of care (as reflected in JCAHO and NC A standards).[1] Locally based integrated delivery systems can't afford the time, cost and effort to spoon feed standards of care or criteria to independent providers. It is up to the providers to obtain the standards, read and adopt them. The payoffs in being a part of an integrated delivery system is that patients can receive better care with the attention directed to both behavioral and physical health care. As the next century approaches, more emphasis will be placed on the role behavioral healthcare provides in general medical healthcare and how effective behavioral health interventions and approaches can, in fact, impact the escalating cost of medical care. How does the move to quality integrated delivery systems help couples cope better?

E IN C ES C E

As fully integrated systems develop, whether partnerships between providers and hospitals, or health systems run by hospitals, or systems owned by other healthcare entities, the opportunities will be available for treating couples as whole families or treating the whole person which will result in the best overall healthcare. While these newer healthcare systems gain strength and go after insurance business and/ or private employer business as well as public sector business, they can offer a complete package of all services at rates which are attractive to the payers. As provider incentives or reimbursement systems move to capitation and subcapitation models where a full amount of money is paid in advance each month for each covered member or covered life, then the budgeting process of where dollars get put in treatment becomes the responsibility of the fully integrated system. In such a system, the early identification of individuals and couples having behavioral problems that could lead to more costly healthcare or mental healthcare becomes the primary goal for longer term medical or treatment cost savings. As research has shown, stress and behavioral dysfunctions can lead to or exacerbate medical conditions; it only makes sense that early behavioral interventions offered in a single provider based health system will be used to prevent more serious medical problems. In this future-oriented, quality based and integrated care paradigm, physicians or other providers in the medical system can identify individual and couples problems and quickly refer them (without worrying about extra costs) within the system for resolution by a behavioral health professional. Sharing in cost savings, physicians and the health system are better incentivized for appropriate involvement of behavioral healthcare. Thus, in the fully integrated system, couples will better be able to cope, if all of their healthcare and relationship problems that can precipitate more serious health problems are handled by an organization that is at-risk for all of the care for the individual. In many parts of the country there has been rapid development of integrated delivery systems that offer all care from birth of an infant to providing senior nursing/medical care within the same system. Independent providers who will be practicing in ten, fifteen or twenty years need to develop an alignment with an integrated delivery system in order to be involved in both public and private sector funding in the future. For continuation of reimbursed treatment to better help couples cope in the future such participation is essential. There will always be opportunities for some providers who choose to seek patients who will self-pay for services, but with the surplus of providers the competition will be far too great for most to survive. For many patients the cost of couples' treatment without benefit coverage adds an additional financial strain on whatever stresses are already contributing to the couple's problems. In the future, an important screening tool will be used by physicians (or other entry point individual professionals) who first see patients, couples or families at the first point of contact. With such screening, referrals will quickly be made to a provider who can treat the problems, whether or not the presenting problems are those that meet "reimbursable" diagnoses. To sum, with the "one stop" shopping in a fully integrated system, the opportunities to help couple's cope would be greater without any additional financial or other stresses put on the couple. In addition, traditionally, non-reimbursed preventive or educational support programs will be more available as they can result in greater savings in treatment costs to the single system.

C NC SI N

Managed care as it is now practiced, is an incredible stressor to individual providers and patients alike. Professional organizations and providers continue to complain about managed care of the present and have been putting energy into trying to pass legislation to set up review-er standards and any willing provider networks. The complaining and legislation will still not resolve the problem of treating the individual or the family as a whole. Even if such laws pass, the in the short run, the larger managed care organizations will find loopholes in the rules and regulations and patients will still not get needed care. The emphasis of focusing on the current managed care or terrorist paradigm, which is already shifting, is a sorrowful waste of resources. Providers need to focus on where the future is moving in this industry, i.e., quality, posi-tive relationships with payers, and the integration of MH/CD services with healthcare services. Lobbying to include couples treatment in cur-rent benefit plans may be too little too late for the current managed care paradigm. Emphasis needs to be placed on including couple's treatment as a part of a larger healthcare plan or program offered by provider-based systems that are gearing up to cut out the middlemen (current payers, utilization reviewers and benefit controllers). When hospitals and providers create systems which are cost effective and risk bearing, don't require overseers and do align provider incentives, then managed care, as it is practiced now, will disappear.

In sum, the answer to the question "How does managed care help couples cope?" is, for the time being, it doesn't! The real question for providers to answer is "what can we do to make managed care be-come more relevant to help couples cope?" And the solution is, to give up fighting managed care terrorism and move to the next para-digm. In moving to a new paradigm, those who are the early paradigm pioneers will professionally outlive and outlast those who remain paralyzed in the current paradigm.

A THOR NOTE

Following six years as a mental health administrator for the Ohio Department of Mental Health, James M. Shulman began a full-time solo private practice in 1980 working with couples and families. The practice flourished by learning how to work in a managed care environment and in 1997 was acquired by Mount Carmel Health System, a Columbus Ohio healthcare system with three hospitals. Dr. Shulman holds a PhD in Clinical Psychology from the University of Montana (1973), is a past President of the Ohio Psychological Association (1986-87) and a national speaker on quality practice and innovative behavioral healthcare delivery systems.

NOTE

1. Standards are available from NC A, 2000 . St. NW. Ste 00. Washington. D.C. 20036 and JCAHO, One enaissance oulevard. Oak rook Terrace. Illinois 60181.

REFERENCES

Austad, C. (1996). *Is Long Term Psychotherapy Unethical* San Francisco: Jossey-ass Publishers.
Cummings, N., Pallak, M. and Cummings, J. (1996). *Surviving the Demise of Solo Practice: Mental Health Practitioners Prospering in the Era of Managed Care.* Madison, Connecticut: Psychosocial Press.
Feldman, S. (1992). *Managed Mental Health Services.* Springfield, Illinois: Charles C. Thomas Publisher.
Modern Healthcare (8 97) Chicago: Crain Publications.
Shulman, J. (1993). Managed Care, Terrorism and Paradigm Shifts in ehavioral Healthcare. *The Independent Practitioner,* 1 (2), 38-39.
Shulman, J. (199). Dealing with the City or Uncertainty of Overcoming the Future Neuroses. *The Independent Practitioner,* 1 (3), 121-122.
Shulman, J. (1996). Forecasting the Niche Market. *The Independent Practitioner,* 16(2), 92-93.
Winegar, N. (1992). *The Clinician's Guide to Managed Mental Health Care.* New ork: The Haworth Press, Inc.

Comment:
How Managed Care
Can Help Couples Cope

Alma I. Silverthorn

SUMMARY. omments on the role of greed at all levels of the managed care system, from individual patients to corporations. t is suggested that couples therapists not seek inclusion as "health care providers." *[Article copies availa le for a fee from The Haworth Document Delivery Service: 8 34 678. E mail address: getinfo haworthpressinc.com e site: http: www.haworthpressinc.com*

KEYWORDS. Managed care, uality, greed, capitation

My initial reaction to the title of the preceding article was: Satire? Delusion? Or Lie? The answer was none of the above. It is an accurate description of the current state of managed care and couples therapy. It is also an accurate, though limited, history of how we got here. Beginning with "Crystal Balling the Future . . ." most of the changes being proposed for the general health care system are covered quite clearly. I do not share the author's optimism that these will provide good health care, or be expanded to cover couples therapy. He overlooks, or at least doesn't mention, one critical variable. Greed!

Managed care arose to counter rising health costs. A large factor in those high costs was greed of the practitioner, who also cared about

---

Alma I. Silverthorn, PhD, is recently retired from private practice and is on the Editorial oard of the *Journal of Couples Therapy.*

[Haworth co-indexing entry note]: "Comment: How Managed Care Can Help Couples Cope." Silverthorn, Alma I. Co-published simultaneously in *Journal of Couples Therapy* (The Haworth Press, Inc.) Vol. 8, No. 3/4, 1999, pp. 8 -89; and: *Couples Therapy in Managed Care: Facing the Crisis* (ed: Barbara Jo Brothers) The Haworth Press, Inc., 1999, pp. 8 -89. Single or multiple copies of this article are available for a fee from The Haworth ocument elivery Service [1-8 -34 -9 8,9: a.m. - 5: p.m. (ST). -mail address: getinfo haworthpressinc.com].

87

the patients. Now it becomes undiluted greed. A basic fact is that managed care programs for both physical and mental health are public corporations or subsidiaries of insurance companies that trade on the stock market, and the price of their shares have done exceptionally well. That is because their profits have been outstanding, and people with money love that. As an investor (not in managed care companies), I know this from personal experience. These companies are here to stay, as long as the profit margin continues.

In the public arena, Medicare and Medicaid policies are established by Congress, and somewhere along the line State politicians get to have input. As the ongoing machinations over campaign financing highlights, those with money get access to attempt to influence the decisions made by our elected representatives at all levels. This is not going to change.

Ross Perot's fortunes increased substantially during the time one of his companies was involved with the administration of MediCal (the California title of Medicaid) benefits and claims. Contracting with governments to provide any kind of service is a lucrative business and will continue to be. I do not expect to see "greater built in controls."

Companies who provide health benefits to their employees want the most they can get for the least cost. Individuals want insurance coverage for the least premium, and it is mostly when they need a service not covered that they become unhappy.

Integrated delivery systems that are forming are subject to the bottom line, "less expensive" rather that "better quality." Among the many new ventures "preparing for the future" in California, I know of at least one that hired a new administrator as a part of the process. She decided to remove new, more expensive medications for schizophrenia from the drug sample room, on the basis that older, cheaper medications such as Haldol are preferable. The fact that the new medications have fewer side effects are irrelevant, the important issue was that the group be profitable.

With capitation, if you treat one individual with an expensive medication or couples therapy, you have to hope the rest of the people you see that day will only be complaining of the common cold, and that lots of folks won't get sick at all. I am not optimistic that as fully integrated systems develop, there will be many who will take the opportunity to treat couples as whole families with the overall best health care.

Neither from my prospective as a psychotherapist, nor as someone who needs health care from time to time, do I see anything nearly as rosy as pictured in the article. As a therapist I have learned to listen and look at what is going on behind the verbiage. I am not implying that the author originated this bull . . . , I think he or she has probably bought into the popular paradigm. In the short run, meaning the next 2 or so years, this situation is going to get worse. I think, ultimately, when enough of us so called "consumers of health care" become angry enough, we may begin to recognize that health care is a right, not a privilege. In the meantime, I would suggest that couples therapists not rush to become part of "health care," but find ways to establish a practice outside the system and expect that their clients will have to pay out of pocket. This, of course, means that the poorer and sometimes more desperately in need couples won't receive services. That is the way things work now.

Rejoinder to: "How Managed Care Can Help Couples Cope"

Joseph A. Cattano

INTR D CTI N

This article, ostensibly a discussion on the impact of managed care upon the provision of couples therapy, more accurately is a "venting" of the author's anger and an expression of his dismay pertaining to the more egregious aspects of working in a managed behavioral health care environment. nfortunately, it is also a rather blatant and vitriolic "assault" on his fellow practitioners for being, in some misconstrued manner, the agents that have brought this "blight" upon our profession. Moreover, it is glaringly apparent that the author has significant misconceptions and misperceptions pertaining to the origins and nature of managed care. It is these misunderstandings that l will attempt to address in this brief discussion.

ANA ED CARE T E REA RI INS

The author clearly describes the "Age of Freedom" (Shulman, p. 78) and the significant expansion in the provision of psychotherapeutic

---

Joseph A. Cattano is in private practice.

Address correspondence to: Joseph A. Cattano, PhD, 36 East Woodbine Drive, Freeport, N   11 20.

[Haworth co-indexing entry note]: " e oinder to: 'How Managed Care Can Help Couples Cope.'" Cattano, Joseph A. Co-published simultaneously in *Journal of Couples Therapy* (The Haworth Press, Inc.) Vol. 8, No. 3/4, 1999, pp. 91-1   ; and: *Couples Therapy in Managed Care: Facing the Crisis* (ed: Barbara Jo Brothers) The Haworth Press, Inc., 1999, pp. 91-1 . Single or multiple copies of this article are available for a fee from The Haworth ocument elivery Service [1-8 -34 -9 8, 9:   a.m. - 5:   p.m. (ST). -mail address: getinfo haworthpressinc.com].

services that occurred in the period of the 197 s through the 198 s. Psychotherapists, much to their credit, surely spearheaded the effort to have healthcare benefits extended to cover consumers in need of mental health services. I suggest that the author is accurate in describing both the proliferation and ease of availability of services that characterized this period. Surely, in no small measure, these changes were ushered in by the addition of mental health coverage to many healthcare policies. l further suggest that there is validity in his criticism that this period witnessed the overuse particularly of both inpatient adolescent psychiatric hospitalizations and inpatient stays for substance abuse and alcoholism detoxification (Shulman, p. 78). There is little question that these frequent and overly long stays were, in some cases, economically motivated. However, l believe that he should consider the following issues.

First, the notion that these apparent abuses resulted in the emergence of managed behavioral care (Shulman, p. 77) is unfounded. Clearly, in the late 198 s and the 199 s, we experienced skyrocketing healthcare insurance premiums. However, I suggest that the notion that managed healthcare came into being as a response to and cure for these rapidly escalating costs is only partially accurate (Gumpert Kagan, 1997). It is my opinion that managed care, although cleverly marketed as a panacea, is first and foremost a *siness strategy* that enabled corporations to gain access to approximately seventeen percent of the Gross National Product (GNP). Shrewd business minds recognized that the current economic and business climate pertaining to the provision of healthcare offered an opportunity to develop and market a product (managed care) that would enable them to tap into the sizable percentage of the GNP that was being spent on healthcare, thereby creating the potential for securing huge profits. What I am suggesting is that a calculated and rather ruthless "takeover" of healthcare was cleverly disguised and presented to the consumer, businessman, and legislator as a "rescue"–saving businesses from potentially financially ruinous annual healthcare premiums.

Surely, we professionals bear considerable responsibility for opening the gates to the "wolves," as we were not fully appreciative of the impact escalating premium costs had on businesses in an employer-based system for the purchasing of healthcare. In this regard, we surely fueled the engines of the managed care industry and created unnecessary distance between us and the employer. Although, it is interesting to note that the healthcare industry and certain providers were gradually beginning to put into place various controls on costs, primarily through the use of *esignate rate g i es* (DRGs). DRGs were becoming quite successful both in limiting length of stay for specific hospital procedures and in establishing reasonable and standardized rates of reimbursement. So, there was evidenced a beginning awareness of the need to control healthcare costs. However, we must understand that it was not simply the increased cost from the providers that was solely the problem. The cost of *health ins ran e* was skyrocketing! We must be cautious here, as too often we confuse the cost of healthcare insurance with the actual cost of healthcare services. I suggest that we may have naively assumed that changes in the cost of health insurance are a direct reflection of actual increases in cost of services provided. One is not necessarily a reflection of the other. It is interesting to conjecture that what we may have experienced in the past decade is a dramatic double-digit increase in the cost of *health are ins ran e*, which may be quite far removed from the actual increase in the cost of the services provided to the consumer. Managed care promised to stop these rapidly escalating costs of healthcare insurance through utilization review, provider panels, and controlling the healthcare marketplace. And of course, all of this would be accomplished without sacrificing quality!

Second, the author appears quite concerned and somewhat indignant about the *e esses* of providers during the "Age of Freedom"; yet, he fails to address the *e essi e* profits and corporate executive salaries that are currently being evidenced in the health insurance/ managed care industry. *Mo ern ealth are* (April 6, 1998, p. 16) reported: "Richard Scrushy, HealthSouth Corporation's chairman and chief operating executive officer earned more than 12 *million* in salary, bonus, stock options and other compensation last year." This same industry weekly (April 6, 1998, p. 6) further cited Representative Charles Norwood (R-Ga.) pertaining to the outrageous salaries HMO executives are currently earning, yet at the same time clamoring for increases in premiums and reduction in services. Norwood states: "For top-level HMO executives to make millions upon millions may be OK. . . . But when they complain about pennies for patient protection, that is pure hypocrisy." It appears that some are very concerned about the increasing cost of healthcare, yet, they turn their heads away from seeing the outrageous plunder of the consumers' and corporations' premium dollars that are being spent on these incredible salaries.

ANA ED E A I RA   EA T CARE

I must take umbrage with the author when he infers that mental healthcare professionals took advantage of the situation provided during the "Golden Age" for the sake of personal financial aggrandizement (p. 76-77). As is usually the case, some practitioners did misuse the generous climate of the past few decades. However, I am confident in my belief that most instances of excess were in the service of cautiousness and conscientiousness. The author fails to understand that the advent of managed behavioral healthcare was a natural extension of that phenomenon which was already occurring in traditional physical healthcare. Managed behavioral healthcare came into being because there was significant profit in micro-management of treatment and utilization review; simply, it was a natural extension of that which was taking place in other aspects of healthcare. Moreover, no one seemed prepared to counter it. In an employer-based system for purchasing healthcare insurance, employers determined both the providers/insurers and the package of benefits to be offered to employees. Smart marketing companies promised businesses significant savings in mental health care while assuring them that there would be no decline in services or the quality of treatment; simply, they would just "remove the fat and excess." Employers, ever conscious of enhancing profits, bought these cleverly marketed packages. nfortunately, what they did not realize was that they could accomplish the same outcome without the costly managed care middle-man simply by imposing restrictions on mental/behavioral health care services through annual "caps" on reimbursement and number of sessions. Moreover, what was not recognized in this "rush" to manage behavioral healthcare was the fact that outpatient mental health treatment has always been cost effective and self-limiting. Patients often stay fewer than ten sessions, usually experiencing enough relief from distress to terminate treatment. Those that stay longer do so because there is a genuine need (Bak Weiner Jackson, 1992). Most mental health practitioners traditionally exercised a "sort of" self management of their practices. They are well aware of the competitive nature of practice and restrain themselves from pricing themselves out of the market. Again, the problem in behavioral healthcare was almost exclusively in the area of inpatient adolescent treatment and inpatient substance abuse treatment. But managed care companies convinced employers that all aspects of mental health services were out of control in order to solidify their position. The result was that a new industry was born, situating itself between the patient and the provider and able to absorb significant premium dollars–dollars that could be better spent in the provision of needed services.

AN   ED CARE

In describing the "Reign of Terror," the author presents a credible description of some of the more egregious aspects of practicing in a mental health environment. He states:

> Despite the original intent of managed care plans, much of the initial efforts by insurers and their agents really focused on managing costs and rationing care rather than on managing care . . . providers felt terrorized by payers, and what was called managed care was more often described as mismanaged or "mangled care." Payers and their agents cut fees, held providers hostage to contract language, e.g., with gag rules, denied care, outright refusal or delayed payments and threatened providers who would not follow rules. (Shulman, p. 78)

However, once again, the author seems quick to take the side of managed care and blame the providers. He states: " nfortunately, managed behavioral health care plans had some legitimacy in distrusting providers as many remained unfocused on their treatment, continued unnecessary utilization, kept poor or no (legally required) records and acted as if insurance coverage was an entitlement" (Shulman, p. 8). I wish to take exception to these comments. First, what does he mean by "unfocused?" My opinion is that he might be referring to any modality other than "brief" therapy. Surely, it suggests that psychoanalytic treatment might fall into this category of "unfocused" treatment. Second, what is being inferred by the author with the notion of "unnecessary utilization?" I guess that would depend upon who is determining the efficacy of treatment–a company reviewer or the provider. Third, insurance coverage *is* an entitlement! It is given to employees as part of a total reimbursement package and is a benefit in lieu of direct salary. It is not a favor or gift granted by the employer out of the goodness of their heart–as it is often depicted by management. Rather, it is part of the cost of their services as employees. Lastly, the author has repeatedly referred to the poor record keeping practices of mental health practitioners. In my opinion, most mental health practitioners are reluctant to maintain extensive and detailed records, as the nature of the material they deal with is often exquisitely sensitive. Surely, these concerns are justified in today's electronic computerized data world, as it is well documented that the confidentiality of patient records has been severely compromised–if not destroyed.

INTE RATED DE I ER S STE S

The author presents Integrated Delivery Systems (IDS) as the heir apparent to today's managed care debacle. Clearly, he is favorable to this "supposedly" new approach to the delivery of healthcare, as he suggests that it combines quality with cost consciousness. He states:

> These provider systems negotiate preferred or exclusive arrangements with payers and seek partnerships that both focus on quality and align incentives through risk sharing models rather than accepting lower and lower fee-for-service amounts. In the behavioral health arena systems negotiate case rates to provide all services for certain diagnostic groups or agree to subcapitation rates for behavioral health services. Driven by the accreditation standards National Committee for uality Assurance (NC A), payers are seeking the providers who can best meet the standards, demonstrate quality or performance improvement, can service the whole patient and at the same time can provide required data and reports to support these efforts. (Shulman, p. 82).

Once again, the author either cannot or elects not to see the sordid nature of these various schemes. l am afraid that in many respect, IDS is nothing more than "old wine in a new bottle"–and not a very good vintage at that! It is essential to realize that IDS is built upon the notions of case fees and/or capitation as the means for reimbursing professional providers for services rendered. It is my contention that these two concepts are far more dangerous to the welfare of the patient and quality treatment than utilization review is in its most noxious form. It is important to recognize that with case fees and capitation, the "bloody knife" has been passed from the case manager and reviewer to the provider. Managed care companies and insurers/payers can conveniently both "wash their hands" of any wrongdoing for denying services as that decision now rests with the provider and all but eliminate the expense of utilization review. In essence, the concept of risk has been shifted, for the most part, to the provider of services. The reality is that the patient is now in an adversarial position with the provider, as his/her healthcare needs are a direct threat to the financial solvency and well-being of the provider and his/her organization. Each session, each procedure drains the monies that the provider needs to retain as income/profit. It is a delivery design that clearly highlights the fact that healthcare is rapidly becoming nothing more than a commodity–not unlike soybeans and hog bellies–to be dealt and manipulated so as to insure the highest profit. In this type of environment *ality an not e ist* Dr. Ivan Miller addresses these concerns:

> Integrated delivery systems are the latest disguise of managed care. The proponents of these systems claim that patients will get the best mental health services of the primary care physician and the mental health professional are in the same office and are funded by the same pool of funds. Although these proponents claim to be focused primarily on the patient's best interest, a careful review of the finding arrangements shows that these systems are really driven by the financial principles of managed care: funds are capitated and prepaid, proprietary secrecy hides how much money is diverted to administration and profit, and those who deny treatment get to pocket the funds entrusted for patient services. (Miller, 1998, p. 9)

C NC SI N

It is my opinion that the author is either somewhat misinformed or not truly desirous of understanding the reality of managed care. There is no question that there were excesses in the traditional fee-for-service system resulting in overutilization and greater expense than what may have been objectively justified. Equally, there is no question that diligent management of healthcare services can be beneficial in containing certain costs and assisting in curtailing overutilization and unnecessary procedures. However, the commitment to the concepts of improving care and guaranteeing quality must prevail in any system that has the capacity to influence and/or override the clinical judgement of healthcare providers. In a for-profit system that foremost has an unyielding allegiance to profit, shareholder dividends, and market share, patient well-being and quality of care become expensive afterthoughts. Simply, patients end up getting shortchanged; tragically, too many are physically and psychologically harmed.

However, there is a strong change in the tide witnessed in recent months. Throughout the country, managed care is falling into disfavor–even with politicians. Legislation is pending or has been already passed in many states that safeguards consumers from some of the more egregious practices of managed care. On a federal level, Sen. Alphonse D'Amato (R-NY) and Rep. Charles Norwood (R-Ga.) have cosponsored the Patient Access to Responsible Healthcare Act (PAR-CA), a bill that is receiving considerable bipartisan support (Chiaramonte, 1998). This legislation is representative of the backlash that is building pertaining to managed care as consumers are becoming more demanding of legislative regulations and less tolerant of abusive policies. This is being evidenced in many medicare HMOs, as those patients in need of specialists or highly skilled procedures will often disenroll from their respective HMOs in order to access the specialist of their choice (CSPAN2, 1998). Today, many consumers and employers seeking choice, access and affordability, are electing to enroll with various PPOs instead of HMOs. A commentary by Bradley Kalish in Modern Healthcare highlights the issue of the waning popularity of managed care HMOs:

> Now that the cost differentials between traditional HMOs and PPOs are insignificant, consumers are less tolerant of the restrictions on choice imposed by the traditional HMO model. One need only read a daily newspaper to feel the heat of the consumer backlash against HMOs . . . Compared with HMOs, PPOs offer less restricted access to physicians, less interference with practitioner practice patterns and a more flexible benefits structure for payers. (Kalish, 1998)

I may be somewhat premature, but managed care *is* dying. It is falling out of favor with most providers and the majority of the

patients that it is supposed to effectively service. The reality of managed care and managed behavioral healthcare is becoming more and
more apparent to all but the most naive observer or the most committed investors. The cost-conscious induced myopia which for so
long has blinded us to the real nature of this beast, is slowly being
corrected and the truth is now quite evident. Bryant Welch, J.D.,
Ph.D., lawyer, psychologist and an acute observer of the healthcare
debacle comments: " . . . managed care was founded on deception
and, as any clinician or patient/victim knows, deception is still the
driving force of the managed care industry the devastation which
managed care has wrought is now permeating the public consciousness" (Welch, 1996).

Of course, the anxiety-proviking question that looms on the horizon
is: "what will replace it in the future?"–as it is very doubtful that we
can ever return to the traditional fee-for-service system of the past.
This question, may in fact, keep managed care in place longer than
necessary, as alternatives are sought. Moreover, the logical choice of a
single payer system has encountered stiff resistance from may quar-
ters, including providers. However, if we are really committed to a
quality health care delivery system, I believe that we will slowly
evolve into the inevitable–a single payer system. This system will not
be a copy of what is in place in Great Britain or Canada, but a uniquely
American system, that may even utilize some aspects of management
of care and utilization review, but within the context of compassion,
quality, and choice.

REFERENCES

ak, J.D.   Weiner, .H. (1992). Managed Mental Health Care Should Independent
Practice Capitulate or Mobili e. *Independent Practitioner*, Part 1, Issue 12.
Carpenter, Margaret   Platt, Sheila (1997). Professional Identity for Clinical Social
Workers: Impact of Changes in Health Care Delivery Systems. *Clinical Social
ork Journal   olume 5 Num er 3   all   7*, p. 338.
Chiaramonte, John (1998). Vendorship   Managed Care. *The Clinician Newsletter
of the New York State Society for Clinical Social   ork Inc.* Winter 1998, Vol. 29,
No. 1, p. .
For the   ecord. *Modern Healthcare*, April 6, 1998, p. 16.
umpert, Peter   Dagan, Daniel (1997). AMHA Manages Costs . . . ut it is *not*
Managed Care. *Coalition Report The National Coalition of Mental Health Pro
fessionals and Consumers Inc.*, March 1 , 1997, p. 1.
alish,   radley (1998). Commentary. *Modern Healthcare*, April 20, 1998, p. 96.

Miller, Ivan (1998). The New Face of Managed Care–Integrated Delivery Systems. *Coalition Report The National Coalition of Mental Health Professionals and Consumers Inc.*, March 1998, p. 9.

Welch, ryant (1996). The Death of Managed Care. *Coalition Report The National Coalition of Mental Health Professionals and Consumers Inc.*, November 1 , 1996, p. 1.

Wissenstein, Eric (1998). Survey Cites HMO Exec s High Pay. *Modern Healthcare*, April 6, p. 6.

Singing Our Own Song

Howard Halpern

SUMMARY. The demands of managed care and concurrent trends in our society challenge us to assert the crucial role of treating relationships and of pursuing the development of deepened self understanding in our patients and ourselves. n the name of speed, efficiency and cost containment too much that is healing can be undervalued and unreimbursed. e must find ways to facilitate change in our patients through the treatment of their important relationships and through encouraging them to take the time for sensitive self confrontation and e ploration. *Article copies availa le for a fee from The Haworth Document Delivery Ser vice: 8 34 678. E mail address: getinfo haworthpressinc.com e site: http: www.haworthpressinc.com*

KEYWORDS. Third party payers, managed care, relationships, growth

Fifteen years ago, I began my book *ow to reak o r i tion to a erson*, with these words:

Maybe the Surgeon General hasn't determined it yet, but staying in a bad relationship may be dangerous to your health. It can shake your self esteem and destroy your self confidence as surely

---

Howard Halpern, PhD, has focused on turning disturbed relationships into gratifying ones in over four decades of work as a psychotherapist. This interest has been reflected in many articles and five books including *Cutting Loose: An Adult Guide to Coming to Terms with Your Parents How to Break Your Addiction to a Person* and *inally Getting It Right: rom Addictive Love to the Real Thing.* He has served as president of the American Academy of Psychotherapists.

[Haworth co-indexing entry note]: "Singing ur wn Song." Halpern, Howard. Co-published simultaneously in *Journal of Couples Therapy* (The Haworth Press, Inc.) Vol. 8, No. 3/4, 1999, pp. 1 1-1 ; and: *Couples Therapy in Managed Care: Facing the Crisis* (ed: Barbara Jo Brothers) The Haworth Press, Inc., 1999, pp. 1 1-1 . Single or multiple copies of this article are available for a fee from The Haworth ocument elivery Service [1-8 -34 -9 8, 9: a.m. - 5: p.m. (ST). -mail address: getinfo haworthpressinc. com].

as smoking can damage your lungs. When people say that their relationship with their partner–a lover or spouse–is killing them, it may be true. The tensions and chemical changes caused by stress can throw any of your organ systems out of kilter, can drain your energy, and lower your resistance to all manner of unfriendly bugs. And often it can drive one to the overuse of unhealthy escapes, such as alcohol, amphetamines, barbiturates, narcotics, tranquilizers, reckless pursuits, and even overt suicidal acts.

The aim of that paragraph was primarily to focus the reader on the pernicious effects of destructive relationships not only on his state of mind but his state of health. Besides this, I had a secondary goal. From experiences I had begun to have with insurance companies who purported to "cover" psychotherapy expenses motivated me to want to tell third-party payers that relationship disorders presented a serious threat to bodily wellbeing. I presented this illness-based argument not only because it was true but because I was concerned about the tendencies to downplay and even invalidate the importance of treating the emotional pain, frustration and demoralization suffered in bad relationships unless it was directly related to medical symptomatology and individual diagnosis. As far as I can see, we are still nowhere near the point where under "name of patient" on most insurance or managed care forms we can write, "the relationship between Harry and Sally" or the relationships between "Harry, Sally and Harry, Jr." It would not fit the usual medical model. This is not to say that we do not treat relationships, but we and our patients can be subtly coerced to focus on the clinical symptomatology rather than the factors in significant relationships that nourish those symptoms. And when the focus is in fact on these relationships, we all know of incidents where therapists who are seeing a couple or family list only one member as a patient on required forms in order to make reimbursement more certain. In other words, there is often pressure, direct or not, for the therapist to be untruthful in telling insurance and managed care entrepreneurs what the type of treatment is, even when the therapist has determined that treatment to be in the best interest of the patient. (One therapist who was reporting her treatment of her patient's destructive relationship with her husband was told, "We're not paying for you to be Dear Abby!") And can these therapists be sure that this clerical untruth does not influence his and his patient's perception and approach to the treatment?

Besides the understandable tendency for medical plans to emphasize a medical model, managed care, in itself and *as part o other so ietal tren s*, has influenced the practice of psychotherapy in two ways that I find particularly distressing. The first, as just discussed, is to devalue the treatment of relationships (the horizontal dimension). The other is to underemphasize the pursuit of self awareness (the vertical dimension) as a route to a fuller and healthier life. There is little patience with promoting deepened self-knowledge, including insight into unconscious processes such as hidden impulses, repressed memories, dream messages, disowned feelings and denied motivations. This vertical dimension has long been recognized as a frequent and often necessary prerequisite to change but it is inefficient in time and money terms. I have no doubt that managed care would reimburse this pursuit of self-awareness if it were effective in producing salutary changes in just a few visits. But that is not the time frame in which insight oriented therapy usually works. The process of converting insight into change takes time, often lots of time. Painful insights are warded off as part of a misguided self-protective process (as Hermann Hesse says in *aemion*, "There is no path so distasteful to a man than the path that leads to himself").

Second, once the insight is gained and accepted, changing long entrenched patterns of thinking, feeling and behaving is like trying to turn around a huge ocean liner in a narrow channel–it takes enormous patience, painstaking maneuvering, much backing and forthing, and the ever present danger of getting stuck and of foundering. Is this something managed care would want to pay for? Is it something that they should pay for? And even with the studies that show that the success of psychotherapy is positively correlated with the amount of time spent in it, is it something that managed care providers and insurance companies can feasibly pay for?

There is a wonderful depiction of the differing goals of insurance companies and providers in the novel *Mo nt Misery* by Samuel Shem in which the psychiatrist protagonist is questioned about his treatment of his patient, Christine.

> She had gotten a lot better, and since she was a young-sounding woman–a girl, really–her "case manager" in Tulsa who demanded to know increasingly personal details about Christine: Was she having sex with her boyfriend? If she was depressed, why wasn't she on drugs? Couldn't it all be PMS?

On the basis of my answers, the teenybopper in Tulsa would authorize another two sessions at a time. it was infuriating. One day I said to her:

"You're making it impossible for me to do psychotherapy with her."

"Yeah, I know," the girl said, her chewing gum snapping loudly. "We don't like to pay for psychiatrists to talk to people anymore."

"What do you mean?"

"We onny pay psychiatrists to hand out drugs."

"Well, who the hell are people supposed to talk to?"

"Gotta putchu on hold."

I fought; the girl in Tulsa won. Christine's insurance no longer paid for therapy.

The tendency of third-party payers not to support long-term treatment (of individuals or relationships) will doubtless grow. Cost-benefit analyses will increasingly prompt them to support the use of medication and symptom-oriented therapy instead. This has already contributed to a change in the mindset, expectations and goals of patients and prospective patients. But it is crucial to note that it is not the prevalence of managed care insurance companies alone that has caused enormous changes in attitudes toward and practice of psychotherapy. In the forty-five plus years since I met with my first psychotherapy patient (in a V.A. Hospital) earthquakes have occurred in the way we all experience ourselves in the world. Soon after I started my own analytic training in the early 195 s, I remember discussing with one of my first "control analysts" (which is what we called supervisors in that time and place) the "rule" that patients were to make no life changing major decisions until their analysis was complete. She explained, "in the early days of psychoanalysis, when analyses lasted five months and marriages lasted fifty years such a rule made sense. But now that marriages last five years and analyses last fifty years it does not." The increasing duration of intensive psychotherapy reflected a commitment to deep, full and profound self awareness. (In my crowd going to therapy less than three times a week was considered superficial.) At the same time, the trend toward more quickly broken marriages reflected and were part of other social and experiential seismic shifts that continue to this time. They were part of a ubiquitous trend toward an accelerating velocity of experiences and expectations, always in the service of increased efficiency and a speedier elimination of frustration. Fast food, supersonic travel, T.V. sound bites, E-mail and other forms of instant communications have created a zeitgeist that promotes shallower, more disposable relationships (between marriage partners, lovers, employer and employee, patient and psychotherapist). When there was conflict or dissatisfaction, the goal became a quick fix, an easy solution to often very complex human affairs. This was certainly not a milieu that would prize the unhurried vertical exploration of one's depth or the horizontal exploration of and taking responsibility for one's relationships.

These societal changes in themselves would be enough to impact the pace and goals of psychotherapy, but in addition there were upheavals in the mental health field itself. Halfway through my first year of internship (1951-1952), in the locked wards of a psychiatric hospital, two anti-psychotic medications (thorazine and rauwolfia serpentina) were introduced in that facility. Despite my youthful commitment to the psychological origins of all mental illness and therefore to psychological approaches to cure, I could not help but be impressed by the dramatic transformation of the snake pit bedlam that characterized many wards to a calmer atmosphere with less violent, more rational, accessible and confrontable patients. That was the beginning of the psychopharmacological revolution that has transformed the way many psychiatric disorders, discomforts and dysfunctions are now, at least in part, treated.

There were other changes that directly influenced the practice of contemporary psychotherapy. There was the expansion of self-help groups of all types, the weekend workshops that promised to change your life in forty-eight hours or simply offered a place to deal openly and directly with your issues. There were the self-help books that ranged from the tritely simplistic to genuine attempts to offer the benefits of current knowledge in a useful form. And there was the beginnings of the notion that a third-party–someone other than the patient–should pay towards the treatment. I remember that moment several decades ago when a patient first handed me an insurance form. "What's this?" I asked. He told me and I had an uneasy feeling that I had just seen the beginning of boon and a curse. (I had the uneasy premonition that my ownership of my psychotherapist self was in jeopardy.)

All these developments have great value. There is much laudable about efficiency–particularly efficiency in alleviating psychological pain and shifting self-destructive behavior. But we are right to worry that with all this goal-oriented efficiency, the solutions may be superficial and the soul of the patient–whatever that is–unnourished. Not many of our "boomer" patients and still fewer of our "generation   " patients would be excited about Socrates proposition that "the unexamined life is not worth living." And most would look puzzled at Freud's admonition that "a dream unanalyzed is like a letter unopened." Because the nurturing of the soul often takes other ingredients–exquisite empathy, the belief that relationships are precious and must often be the focus of the treatment, the shared belief that self-knowledge is both of value in itself and a catalyst for change and the recognition that the slow unfolding of the process offers much that hasty efficiency does not. When engaged in this effort we can often feel we are engaged in sacred work.

But can we expect institutions charged with responsibilities of cost containment (which must involve limiting the scope and length of treatment) to underwrite our efforts to help patients to live in a more insightful, self-aware and caring way?

Hardly. So while we may have to accept a more situation- and symptom-oriented approach, both because of the limitations of the managed care requirements and because some of our patients will have little interest in depth exploration, there are things we can do. We can do enough work with the underlying core feelings so that our patients can glimpse the relevance and value of self-awareness. We can also try to get each patient to pursue deeper contact with himself and others in additional ways: For example, we can encourage him to keep a personal journal, to note and work on his dreams, to attend relevant workshops and self-help groups and to read books designed to increase self-awareness. We can emphasize that psychotherapy is not just for problem-solving and symptom relief but for, to use John Warkentin's[1] term, "sharpening our growing edge." We can also urge

---

1. Pioneering group therapist in the experiential method. "I have lost interest in 'doing psychotherapy' . . . Now I am more interested in growth" (Warkentin, 1972, p. 243).

patients who have good capacity to grow through intensive and prolonged therapy not to let the treatment be limited by what managed care will pay for but to make an investment in their own growth if they possibly can afford it–the way people did before insurance and managed care.

For me, and for many of us, psychotherapy is the way we sing our song. We must not let managed care or any of the related trends stop us from singing that song. We must sing true to our own rhythms and melodies, not only for our own sake, but as a model to our patients of how they can manage their own care.

REFERENCES

Halpern, H. (1983). *How To Break Your Addiction To A Person.* N : antam, p. 1.
Shem, S. (1979). *Mount Misery.* N : Fawcett, p. 101.
Warkentin (1972). Paradox of being alien and intimate. In A. urton and Associates (Eds.), *Twelve therapists.* San Francisco: Jossey- ass.

Existential Marital Psychotherapy and the Experience of Managed Care

Jim Lantz

SUMMARY. n this article the e perience of managed care is over-viewed from the perspective of e istential marital therapy. t is con-cluded that managed care disrupts the e periential nature of participa-tion between couple and therapist, dilutes the authentic nature of the treatment relationship, decreases the importance of sub ectivity, dis-turbs the discovery of meaning and purpose in marital life and deters e istential communication. *Article copies availa le for a fee from The Haworth Document Delivery Service: 8 34 678. E mail address: getinfo haworthpressinc.com e site: http: www.haworthpressinc.com*

KEYWORDS. Managed care, e istential, systems, authenticity, ethics

Existential marital therapy is a structured helping relationship created for the resolution of disrupted intimacy, meaning and problem-solving in daily marital life (Boerop, 1975; Lantz, 1974, 1994, 1996; Mullan and Sangiuliano, 1964). In existential couples therapy, the treatment process is anchored to five basic existential beliefs: (1) partic-ipation between client couple and therapist should be experiential in nature, (2) the relationship between couple and therapist should be-come an authentic human relationship, (3) the treatment relationship is most important in its subjective element, (4) the discovery of meaning

---

Jim ant , PhD, is Director of the Midwest Existential Psychotherapy Institute, Co-Director of ant and ant Counseling Associates and a Professor at The Ohio State University, College of Social Work, 19 7 College oad, Columbus, OH 3210.

[Haworth co-indexing entry note]: " xistential Marital Psychotherapy and the xperience of Managed Care." ant , Jim. Co-published simultaneously in *Journal of Couples Therapy* (The Haworth Press, Inc.) Vol. 8, No. 3/4, 1999, pp. 1 9-114; and: *Couples Therapy in Managed Care: Facing the Crisis* (ed: Barbara Jo Brothers) The Haworth Press, Inc., 1999, pp. 1 9-114. Single or multiple copies of this article are available for a fee from The Haworth ocument elivery Service [1-8 -34 -9 8, 9: a.m. - 5: p.m. (ST). -mail address: getinfo haworthpressinc.com].

and purpose in life is an important part of marital treatment and (5) only existential communication can facilitate the treatment process (Mullan and Sangiuliano, 1964; Lantz, 1974, 1994, 1996, 1997).

This article will outline my understanding of why existential marital psychotherapy cannot be conducted in a managed care environment. My ideas about this are centered around my view that managed care practice is incompatible with the five central beliefs of existential couples therapy listed above. The remainder of this article will review the incompatibility of each of these five existential beliefs with the managed care reimbursement situation.

E ERIENTIA ARTICI ATI N

Couples frequently come to the treatment situation with fairly rigid ideas and beliefs about how the process of treatment should be "conducted," the role of the psychotherapist and the role of the couple (Lantz, 1974; Mullan and Sangiuliano, 1964). Often such beliefs are constricting and inhibit the very change that the couple hopes to achieve. The constrictions that the couple attempts to place on the psychotherapist can often be understood as a metaphor for the constrictions they place on themselves (Lantz, 1996). In this sense, the therapist's use of experiential and experimental participation to struggle against the couple's attempts at constriction models the freedom and flexibility that are required in functional marital life (Lantz, 1974, 1996; Mullan and Sangiuliano, 1964).

This existential description of experiential participation can be translated into "systems" language by viewing the couple as a closed system, the therapist as an open system and the treatment situation as a system in conflict (Lantz, 1974, 1996). sing systems theory language, there are three potential outcomes in such a conflict treatment situation. First, the couple can teach the therapist to become a closed system. Second, the therapist can teach the couple to become an open system. A final option is for the therapist and couple to terminate their relationship. In existential marital therapy, experimental participation is used by therapist and couple to help them become and remain an open treatment system and to teach them to function more comfortably in an open system manner (Lantz, 1974, 1996, 1997; Mullan and Sangiuliano, 1964).

In the managed care reimbursement situation, there is almost always an attempt by the case manager to get the therapist to identify a psychiatric problem or symptom manifested by the couple and to then identify a procedure used by the therapist *on* the couple to *eliminate* the symptom and/or problem. On the surface, this does not seem a terrible idea; yet from an existential point of view, any attempt to proceduralize the process of treatment constricts therapist and marital flexibility and the couple's freedom to change (Lantz, 1974, 1996; Mullan and Sangiuliano, 1964). The case manager's attempt to develop consistent treatment procedures and protocols inhibits experimental participation and the existential process of change (Lantz, 1994).

A T ENTIC RE ATEDNESS

There is a problematic quality in the relationship between psychotherapist and client couple when either part of the treatment situation aims toward anything other than the lessening of isolation, alienation and the experience of meaninglessness in daily life (Lantz, 1974, 1996; Mullan and Sangiuliano, 1964). nfortunately, many therapists do a great deal to facilitate the continuation of alienation and isolation during the treatment process by relying exclusively upon "techniques," "gimmicks" and "procedures" rather than creative human encounter (Mullan and Sangiuliano, 1964). Although marital psychotherapy demands knowledge, deliberate intervention, timing and evaluation, such technical components must never replace concern, compassion and empathic availability (Lantz, 1974, 1996). sing the terminology of Mullan and Sangiuliano (1964), authentic relatedness must be maintained through a transcendence of preconceived techniques and rigid procedures. sing Marcel's words, this protects the treatment relationship from deteriorating into "technomania" (Lantz, 1996).

In the managed care reimbursement situation, numerous factors work together to disrupt relatedness between the marital therapist and the couple requesting help. The case manager encourages the therapist to utilize treatment techniques to overcome problems, and the exploration of meanings in symptoms and problems between therapist and couple is viewed as "non-specific" and as failing to live up to cost-effective standards of care. In other words, the case manager encourages "I-It" treatment procedures and consistently attempts to disrupt the "I-Thou" tone of the empathic treatment relationship (Lantz, 1996).

S   ECTI IT

There has been considerable pressure in the managed care community to eliminate subjectivity from the treatment process over the past few years. In existential psychotherapy, there is considerable doubt that marital therapy can ever (or should) become a pure, objective science (Lantz, 1996; Mullan and Sangiuliano, 1964). Indeed, subjectivity is not antithetical to the treatment process, but provides opportunities for facilitation of reflection and awareness of the meanings and meaning potentials in daily marital life (Lantz, 1996; Mullan and Sangiuliano, 1964). In existential psychotherapy, it is believed that when the meeting between therapist and the couple becomes merely a "scientific" inquiry, the resulting analytic abstractions will result in the impoverishment of the treatment relationship (Lantz, 1996; Mullan and Sangiuliano, 1964). In existential psychotherapy with couples, subjectivity serves as a pathway to discovery and re-collection of the meanings and meaning potentials in daily marital life (Lantz, 1974; Mullan and Sangiuliano, 1964).

EANIN

In existential psychotherapy (Lantz, 1974, 1996), it is believed that the process of treatment helps the client couple to increase connection, decrease alienation, increase their sense of meaning and purpose in life and, in the words of William Blake, "learn to bear the beams of love." The process of helping couples to increase their awareness of love, fidelity, caring, meaning and concern in the day-to-day occurrences of life has a profound underground connection to a "spiritual faith" (Lantz, 1996). The existential psychotherapist affirms that the concrete experiences of fidelity and meaning in daily life manifest the immanence of god and/or spirituality. To the existential psychotherapist, meaning and love result in an experiential witness to the presence of god and/or spirituality lying at the heart of meaning, fidelity and love. In existential psychotherapy (Lantz, 1996), it is understood that effective treatment often results in awareness of the spiritual light to be found in marital life and a desire for additional reflection about the " ltimate Thou" that such treatment experiences often reveal (Lantz, 1974, 1996).

Such a treatment orientation (focusing upon the exploration of spirituality and meaning awareness) is completely incompatible with the medical model basis of the managed care reimbursement situation. In my view, holding such a treatment orientation and communicating it in any way on a managed care treatment plan will ensure that the therapist will not receive insurance reimbursement for the services he or she has rendered. I am also fairly certain that using such treatment language will often cause the marital psychotherapist to be blacklisted by the managed care insurance agency and/or case management institution (Lantz, 1994).

E ISTENTIA C NICATI N

The central treatment process in an existential treatment approach to marital psychotherapy is the development of existential communication between client couple and psychotherapist providing help (Lantz, 1996). Existential communication occurs when the marital psychotherapist identifies the couple's problem and pain as a human emergency and then accepts this emergency as also present in his/her own self or in his/her own marriage (Lantz, 1974, 1996, 1997; Mullan and Sangiuliano, 1964). In such existential communication, the psychotherapist recognizes that his/her internal pain, which occurs in the presence of the couple, can tell both therapist and couple something important about the couple's existence, something important about the therapist's existence and something meaningful and important about the meaning potentials for growth in the lives of the couple and psychotherapist.

In such existential communication, growth and an expanded sense of meaning and intimacy occur within the total treatment system (Lantz, 1996). Such a process of growth cannot be understood, measured and/or evaluated by most managed care insurance reimbursement systems, and most case managers lack the practice wisdom to understand and/or appreciate the process of treatment that occurs under conditions of existential communication.

A ESTI N STANDARDS

It has been well over ten years since I have accepted reimbursement for marital therapy services from an insurance company. I no longer believe it is ethical to share the kind of information with case managers that the psychotherapist is now requested to share. I do not believe that I should conduct the kind of procedurally based, time-limited forms of treatment that insurance companies now require. I do not wish to talk with a case manager whose loyalty is to the insurance company he/she represents rather than to the couple requesting help. So, I charge a sliding fee. I do not make as much money as my friends who are willing to work in the managed care reimbursement environment. I make less money, my clients pay a bit more money than they would if I accepted managed care reimbursements and both my clients and I use our freedom to decide for ourselves how we will conduct our treatment relationship, how long it will last and what methods we will use.

REFERENCES

oerup, J. (197). Marital therapy: An existential approach. *amily Therapy*, , 269-276.

ant , J. (197). Existential treatment with the Vietnam veteran family. In *Ohio Department of Mental Health yearly report* (pp. 33-36). Columbus: Ohio Department of Mental Health.

ant , J. (199). Ja , art, psychotherapy and the day ob. *oices, 3* , 28-31.

ant , J. (1996). asic concepts in existential psychotherapy with couples and families. *Contemporary amily Therapy, 8*, 3 - 8.

ant , J. (1997). Poetry in existential psychotherapy with couples and families. *Contemporary amily Therapy,* , 371-381.

Mullan, H., Sangiuliano, I. (196). *The therapist's contri ution to the treatment process.* Springfield: Charles C. Thomas.

The Unmanageability
of Characterologic Couples
in Managed Care

Norman F. Shub

SUMMARY. This article e plores the issues associated with treating
characterologic couples in the managed care environment. The article focuses on the definition of the characterologic couple and the specific issues that emerge when the characterologic couple is attempting brief
treatment in the managed care environment. Attention is focused on the
difficulties in the two-stage approach to character treatment, the potential
for hurting the non-characterologic member of the couple, and the problems that emerge when the character is identified, but not worked with.
*Article copies availa le for a fee from The Haworth Document Delivery Ser
vice: 8 34 678. E mail address: getinfo haworthpressinc.com*

KEYWORDS. Managed care, character, rigidity, corpus, iatrogenic

INTR D CTI N

The tongue-twisting nature of this article's title reflects the knotty
problem that has developed during the last several years as couples
struggling with profound and difficult character issues are forced to
address those issues in a managed care environment. Milan (1996)
notes that personality is the most rigid and difficult-to-change element

[Haworth co-indexing entry note]: "The nmanageability of Characterologic Couples in Managed
Care." Shub, Norman F. Co-published simultaneously in *Journal of Couples Therapy* (The Haworth Press,
Inc.) Vol. 8, No. 3/4, 1999, pp. 115-1 4; and: *Couples Therapy in Managed Care: Facing the Crisis* (ed:
Barbara Jo Brothers) The Haworth Press, Inc., 1999, pp. 115-1 4. Single or multiple copies of this article are
available for a fee from The Haworth ocument elivery Service [1-8 -34 -9 8, 9: a.m. - 5: p.m.
(ST). -mail address: getinfo haworthpressinc.com].

of the human self. I prefer the term "character" to "personality" because it better captures the way a person is in the world. The two terms mean much the same thing, however, and Milan and others acknowledge that character is strongly resistant to change because the core traits of characterologic clients are so rigid and because these clients have so few options.

When the difficulty of changing character is combined with the difficulty of changing an intimate system, the problem becomes even more difficult. There are two types of characterologic couples. In the more common type, one person has a rigid character; the other person reacts to that character in a dependent or neurotic way. In the other type, two characterologic people are locked together in some kind of rigid dance. Therapy with either type of couple requires that a character structure be opened before systemic changes can occur. This first principle directly clashes with the philosophy of brief therapy.

T E C ARACTER   IC C   E

A characterologic couple consists of two people, one or both of whose characterologic rigidity defines and organizes the systemic nature of their interactive patterns. The behavioral options of characterologically impaired persons are severely limited in relation to their core traits on a variety of continua–for example, responsibility/irresponsibility, honesty/dishonesty, sensitivity/insensitivity, or willingness to invest in others/disinterest in others.

Sam and Rosita come for marital therapy because Rosita is depressed and complains about Sam's lack of attention and his failure to emotionally connect. They have been married 14 years and have two children, but Rosita always has felt unloved and always has tried to get Sam to give more. At the initial interview, Sam appears robotic, disengaged from his emotional self, and unresponsive to Rosita's feelings.

After several sessions, it becomes clear that Sam has a schizoid character disorder. His character is organized around a group of core traits that lack flexibility. Those traits include sensitivity, insensitivity, investment in self, investment in others, responsibility, irresponsibility, acknowledging and validating feelings, being oblivious to feelings, emotional honesty, and emotional dishonesty. Most people draw upon a variety of behavioral options when confronted with emotional situations, but Sam always is insensitive. He has little flexibility to behave differently in different situations, and of course his behavior drives Rosita to distraction.

Despite Rosita's 14 years of being in a relationship with Sam, where she is getting little and continuously demanding more, he is locked into the fixed nature of his inability to move on the various continua, which we have noted above, and his inability to support her feelings and invest in her in a way that she would be satisfied. Sam's rigidity on each of the continua forms his schizoid personality, and his character structure is organized around his rigid core traits. All Rosita's efforts have been and will be futile. Each of Sam's relationships is the same. His children, his employees, and his minister all report that they cannot get close to him. Everyone acknowledges that Sam is smart, but they remark that he is unemotional and unfeeling and can only care in a distant, robotic way.

In marital therapy, Rosita will complain about Sam's inability to give. However, if the therapy is conducted in a systemic way, regardless of its approach, Sam will not be able to be different. Even if he feels bad, wants to give more, and wants to change the systemic reciprocity, his character must first open up. He doesn't know how to be different and he cannot "will" his behavior to change.

Both Sam's parents were Ph.D. s heavily involved in research and university work who paid little attention to Sam. They sent him to private schools and made sure that his daily life was protected and comfortable, but emotionally they invested almost nothing in him. They did not support his ability to connect with others, encourage him to express his feelings, invest with him on an emotional level, so he had very little idea of the behavioral potential to invest in others. When Sam was sad, they told him to buck up. When Sam had a conflict, they had no time to help him resolve it. When they were struggling or hurting, they never shared their own feelings or demonstrated vulnerability. They did not invest in Sam, nor did they help Sam invest in them or others.

On the sensitivity/insensitivity behavioral continuum, Sam's parents did not help him learn to be sensitive, to care about other people's feelings, or to respond from his heart to emotional situations. So Sam developed narrow options for behavior on that continuum. On the investment in self/disinterest in others continuum, Sam's parents did not work with him, did not share their feelings, and did not talk emotionally to each other or to Sam. They were never openly vulnerable that Sam could remember, so Sam developed few behavioral options on this continuum. On the other continua of character traits that comprise a schizoid personality, the story was similar.

No matter how much Rosita pushed Sam, his characterologic rigidity and his lack of options did not afford him the capacity in his present moment to behave differently toward her. And he was not aware that he had a problem except for what he considered Rosita's incessant complaining. Sam was not in pain and did not suffer. He vaguely realized that he might not have the emotional range of other people, but the thought did not bother him much.

This is the conundrum that characterologic couples pose. Often, in the first type of characterologic couple, the characterologic member is dragged involuntarily into treatment because of the partner's frustration. Rosita and other people in Sam's life constantly tried to get him to be more emotionally responsive, to invest more of his time and energy in them, but they always bumped up against his schizoid personality. Awareness or insight alone will not change behavior. Characterologic couples need to be considered differently.

C ARACTER   ST E ADDRESSED   IRST

For more than 25 years, I have believed and subsequently taught that a therapist's methodology or theoretical framework and whether the therapeutic issues involve a couple, a family, or an organization are not the critical issues when a rigid character structure is involved. The system will organize around the character, and nothing of substance can happen until:

- The rigid character is defined.
- The core traits are clearly visible.
- The character picture (that is, the stylistic way the individual interacts with the environment) is emotionally, intellectually, and affectively owned by the client.
- The core traits have been opened up so that the client has more options to make contact with the environment in moment-to-moment relating.

More evidence has appeared in the last few years to support my belief, but my clinical experience has proven to me that, if a client is characterologically impaired because of a limited number of behavioral options, systems-oriented couples therapy cannot be effective until the client's character is dealt with. I understand that this position is controversial, but this core truth about characterologic people is clear. Accepting the proposition that the client's character must be opened up first means that initially all intimate-systems-oriented therapy must be organized around the character of the characterological member. The client's character must become more flexible so that the client acquires more behavioral options. THEN the systematic therapy, which includes the reciprocity of the couple, has a chance to really work. The couple then can really struggle with changing their intimate system. But character must be dealt with first.

T E I   RTANCE   TI IS
IN TREATIN   T E C ARACTER   IC C   E

For many years, the prevailing attitude in American (perhaps even global) mental health literature has been that characterologic individuals cannot change. Even though interest in treating characterologically impaired clients has grown, our insurance system is set up so that clients with an Axis II diagnosis seldom receive reimbursement. In addition, marital therapy, as we all know, also does not receive reimbursement. So, the combination of the two is a real blockbuster. This situation creates a further problem for treating characterologic couples in managed care. It is true that characterologically impaired clients are among the most difficult to treat. It is also true that the rigid character must be opened up before the system can be addressed. If insurance companies will not pay for marital therapy as well as an Axis II diagnosis, then clinicians who treat characterologic couples are placed in an impossible situation. In a time when our media are filled with reports of teenage violence, gangs, drugs, and other characterologic concerns, the most damaging condemnation of what we are doing as a society is that our own insurance companies will not pay to treat budding characterologic individuals–children, adolescents, and young adults who are struggling with their characters–as well as adults who have already formed rigid characters.

The fact is that character can be changed. (See Shub, 1994 and 1995.) Despite the lack of responsiveness from insurance companies and despite some of the prevailing attitudes that have existed for many years, characterologic individuals are struggling, as are all of us, to attempt to change and grow. They are people whose character has not been supported to become flexible and who have developed rigidity in a group of core traits. A pattern has formed that severely limits their ability to interact and make contact in the world. Once their characters have been opened up so that they have more behavioral options, people with characterologic impairments can transcend their limitations and learn to be different in the world. But before sketching the impact of managed care on characterologic couples, I want to reiterate four important points.

First, one impact of a characterologic member on a system is that the system organizes around the rigid character. Rosita learned not to pressure Sam when she was upset or when he was upset. Because he could not and did not respond, she learned not to share her feelings. She learned not to cry or be sad in front of him. Such behavior would make Sam angry because he did not have the capacity to understand and support it. In general, a characterologic individual's character structure organizes the couple's intimate system. Rosita learned to work around the rigidities of her characterologically impaired husband.

Second, when one or both members of a couple is characterologic, treatment will not be successful until the character becomes more flexible so the person can respond in different ways. Third, characterologic persons often are unaware of the narrowness of their character and thus do not pay much attention to the systemic concerns raised by other members of the system. As a result, their openness to change is limited. Fourth, many therapists do not subscribe to the belief that character must change first and do not have a methodology for addressing character. They may also believe that treating a characterologically impaired person is hopeless. Thus, they tend to subtly advise people who are in an intimate system with a characterologic individual to exit the system.

This fourth issue particularly upsets me. I have seen many situations in which therapists confronted by their own limitations or by the character rigidity of one of a system's members advise (sometimes subtly, sometimes directly) that there is no hope. I find this behavior difficult to understand. I hope that this paper will begin to raise awareness that it is not appropriate to subtly push characterologically impaired couples out of treatment and that characterologically impaired people can change. All that is needed are the appropriate treatment methods to address the character rigidity as a first step.

T E   TI E I   ACTS
ANA ED CARE
N C ARACTER   IC C   ES

I have looked at the two types of characterologic couples, explored the importance of doing character work first to address the client's characterologic rigidity, and examined prevailing attitudes about character. Applying these issues to the managed care environment, it is easy to see why we have a mental health crisis relating to these couples. For both types of characterologic couples, sophisticated treatment is necessary to address character in the first stage of treatment before reciprocity or systemic work can begin in stage two and new patterns of interaction can be successful. I believe that managed care that advocates brief treatment can create additional emotional distress and psychological harm for characterologically impaired couples. In my practice and in my clinical training and teaching experience, I have never seen a couple that has benefitted specifically from brief treatment or managed care approaches when one or both partners was characterologic. In fact, I have consistently seen such couples become casualties of the managed care system. A number of factors contribute to this unfortunate situation.

I   R

Brief treatment often reinforces a client's characterologic rigidity when the character is not addressed first because of economic, time-limitation, or philosophical reasons. Because the treatment is brief, the rigid character cannot be opened up, and new options for behavior on the continua cannot be explored. Thus, there is almost tacit permission for the client to stay the same. And even without tacit permission, the rigidity cannot be resolved. Or perhaps, if confrontation does occur, it may only serve to further rigidify an already rigid character because voicing the systemic concerns without addressing the character first and without creating new options for behavior will usually make no difference. These untreated characterologic clients could not have the ability to behave differently and a confrontation, rather than be helpful, can turn into shaming, blaming, and creating an environment where the characterologic client is encouraged to feel more worthless than hopeful. Brief treatment may many times serves to worsen an already difficult situation, making what is rigid more rigid.

The attitude of insurance companies and the idea held by many mental health professionals that character is untreatable together form an almost total reluctance to acknowledge that character problems even exist. If the existence of such phenomena is not acknowledged, then how can therapists trained by managed care companies in brief-treatment approaches deal with these problems? I have discussed the need for characterologic treatment with many managed care employees and have often heard them say that "We don't do that," or "That's beyond the scope of our policy," or "We don't think that those kind of issues can be treated with psychotherapy." Even though there have been models proffered, literature, and demonstrations of brief treatment for characterologic individuals, this has not seemed to shake the foundation of the managed care company's belief that treating character is not an effective use of psychotherapy dollars. So, from a managed care perspective, the whole subject is imbued with hopelessness by both the managed care agencies and their respective treatment partners.

A I   S   T

Without substantial time and support and without training to understand the complexities of these issues, even sophisticated clinicians are placed in an impossible situation. Treating character is a difficult proposition from any treatment perspective. Therapists are put in a position where they are not supported, trained, or encouraged to do what they need to do to help characterologic couples or to understand their own countertransferential reactions, which makes being a therapist in this environment even more difficult. The countertransferential responses created by an impossible situation can often upset the therapist as well as the couple.

D   D

Finally, the managed care environment often further wounds the non-characterologic system members. They may come to therapy and make themselves vulnerable only to encounter again and again the character rigidity of their partner. Often they need to develop even more defenses to protect themselves from both the ongoing characterologic rigidity of their significant other and the vulnerability they personally experience in the therapy. Many times, the wounds of the individuals in the system have scarred over as protection against the characterologic member's rigidity. When their defenses are opened up again within therapy, further needless wounding may occur. The non-characterologic members may suffer needlessly because not enough time, resources, sophistication, understanding, or optimism are available to help these couples in such situations.

C NC SI N

I am trying to address this issue in terms as strong and clear as possible. I am extremely concerned, as are many others who deal with characterologic couples, that the managed care environment is creating an even grimmer situation than already exists for these couples. Again, this is my position on treating characterologic couples:

1. The character traits of the characterologic members of the system must be addressed first.
2. Therapists must have a methodology of character treatment that helps the person with rigid character become more flexible.
3. If, as in a managed care environment, the resources are not available to support competent treatment of a characterologic impairment, it is likely that the system will become even more dysfunctional *e a se o* the nature of the treatment.

I hope that this article can serve as a wake-up call to practitioners and managed care companies. I apologize for my vehemence, but I have seen many examples of people hurt and wounded by managed care's inability to deal with the needs of characterologic couples.

A THOR NOTE

Norman Shub is an author, teacher, psychotherapist. Norman has been the estalt Institute of Central Ohio s (ICO) director of training since the early 1970 s. nown as a clear and articulate master teacher, Norman s pioneering work in differential diagnosis and the treatment of character disorders has helped develop the understanding that characterologic adults and adolescents can change and benefit from therapy. He is a husband and the proud father of Ariel, his seven-year-old daughter. In addition to books and articles, Norman s current publications include the Working Papers series which is devoted to developing the effectiveness of psychotherapists.

REFERENCES

Abraham,   . (1927). Contributions to the theory of the anal character. In *Selected papers on psychoanalysis*. ondon: Hogarth. (Original work published 1921.)
_____. (1927). Character-formation on the genital level of the libido. In *Selected papers on psychoanalysis*. ondon: Hogarth. (Original work published 192 .)
Akiskal, H. S. (198). Characterologic manifestations of affective disorders: Toward a new conceptuali ation. *Integrative Psychiatry*, , 83-88.
Asperger, H. (19   ). Die autistichen psychopathen im kindesalter. *Archive fur Psy chiatrie und Nerven   rankheiten*, 177, 76-137.
  eck, A. T.,   Freeman, A. (1990b) *Cognitive therapy of personality disorders*. New   ork: uilford.
  lock, J. (1977). Advancing the psychology of personality: Paradigmatic shift or improving the quality of research. In D. Magnusson   N. S. Endler (Eds.), *Personality at the crossroads: Current issues in interactional psychology*. Hillsdale, NJ: Erlbaum.
  uss, D. M.,   Chiodo, . M. (1991). Narcissistic acts in everyday life. *Journal of Personality*, 5 , 179-21 .
Cloninger, C. . (1986). A unified biosocial theory of personality and its role in the development of anxiety states. *Psychiatric Developments*, 3, 167-226.
Eysenck, H. J. (19 2). *The scientific study of personality*. ondon: outledge and   egan Paul.
Frances, A. (198). Validating schi otypal personality disorder: Problems with the schi ophrenia connection. *Schi ophrenia Bulletin*, , 9 - 97.
  underson, J. ., inks, P. S.,   eich, J. H. (1991). Competing models of personality disorders. *Journal of Personality Disorders*, 5, 60-68.
  underson, J. .,   onningstam, E. (1990a, May). Differentiating narcissistic and antisocial personality disorders. Paper presented at the American Psychiatric Association annual convention, os Angeles.
Horney,   . (1939). *New ways in psychoanalysis*. New   ork: Norton.
_____. (19   ). *Our inner conflicts*. New   ork: Norton.
  enrick, D. T.,   Stringfield, D. O. (1980). Personality traits and the eye of the beholder: Crossing some traditional philosophical boundaries in the search for consistency in all of the people. *Psychological Review*, 87, 88-10 .
  iesler, D. J. (1986). The 1982 interpersonal circle: An analysis of DSM-III personality disorders. In T. Millon   . . lerman (Eds.), *Contemporary directions in psychopathology*. New   ork: uilford.
  ivesley, W. J. (1986). Trait and behavioral prototypes of personality disorder. Paper presented at the 138th annual meeting of the American Psychiatric Association (198 , Dallas, Texas). *American Journal of Psychiatry*, 43, 728-732.
Meehl, P. E. (1986). Diagnostic taxa as open concepts: Metatheoretical and statistical questions about reliability and construct validity in the grand strategy of nosological revision. In T. Millon   . itlerman (Eds.), *Contemporary direc tions in psychopathology: Toward the DSM I* (pp. 21 -231). New   ork: uilford.
Milan, T. (1996). *Disorders of personality DSM I : A is II*. New   ork: John Wiley.

Partridge, . E. (1930). Current conceptions of psychopathic personality. *American Journal of Psychiatry*, , 3-99.

Shub, N. (199). *The process of character work: An introduction.* Columbus, OH: estalt Associates, Inc.

_____. (199). The struggles of the characterologic therapist. In M. Sussman (Ed.), *A perilous calling: The ha ards of psychotherapy practice.* New ork: John Wiley.

Index

For Product Safety Concerns and Information please contact our EU
representative GPSR@taylorandfrancis.com Taylor & Francis Verlag GmbH,
Kaufingerstraße 24, 80331 München, Germany

Printed and bound by CPI Group (UK) Ltd, Croydon, CR0 4YY
08/06/2025
01896991-0003